THE MODERN CONSTRUCTION FIRM

Also by Patricia M. Hillebrandt and Jacqueline Cannon

THE CONSTRUCTION COMPANY IN-AND-OUT OF
  RECESSION (*co-author with Peter Lansley*)
THE MANAGEMENT OF CONSTRUCTION FIRMS:
  Aspects of Theory

Also by Patricia Hillebrandt

ANALYSIS OF THE BRITISH CONSTRUCTION INDUSTRY

ECONOMIC THEORY AND THE CONSTRUCTION INDUSTRY

The Modern Construction Firm

Patricia Hillebrandt

and

Jacqueline Cannon

Foreword by W. D. Biggs

MACMILLAN

First edition 1990
Reprinted (with minor corrections) 1994

Published by
THE MACMILLAN PRESS LTD
Houndmills, Basingstoke, Hampshire RG21 2XS
and London
Companies and representatives
throughout the world

ISBN 0–333–46725–6 hardcover
ISBN 0–333–62762–8 paperback

A catalogue record for this book is available
from the British Library.

Printed in Great Britain by
Antony Rowe Ltd
Chippenham, Wiltshire

To our children

Contents

List of Figures

List of Tables

Preface to the 1994 Reprint

In 1986 and 1987 when most of the work was carried out for the two books: *The Management of the Construction Firm: Aspects of Theory* and *The Modern Construction Firm*, the environment in which contractors were operating was one of expanding markets and rising profits. Contractors were increasing their turnover in response to boom conditions, banks were anxious to lend money, most construction companies were involved in property and housing and diversifying into other businesses in the UK and abroad, and all were optimistic about the future.

A third book in the series, *The Construction Company in-and-out of Recession*, which deals with the changes in the environment and the way in which companies have reacted to the worst recession in the construction industry since the Second World War, is to be published. Interviews conducted at the end of 1993 confirmed that companies had shrunk, were retreating into their 'core' businesses and in a few cases were concerned with whether they could survive at all over the period 1994 to 1995. The strategies of the companies in this recessionary environment contrast sharply with those of the earlier period. However, with hindsight it is clear that the seeds of some of the current problems were sown already in 1986 and 1987. The books together provide a unique insight into the dynamics of major construction firms.

Foreword

This volume represents the second part of a major project on the management of construction firms. The first part deals with theory and this one with practice.

The project was undertaken in response to a growing realisation that there existed a gap between technology and management and that, in the field of construction, this gap was perhaps wider than in many other areas.

The Science and Engineering Research Council (SERC) agreed to finance the project as part of its Specially Promoted Programme (SPP) for Research in Construction Management. It was at the time unusual for SERC to support research into areas which are problems in the social sciences. They did so because of the importance of the management of the contracting firm to the whole construction process. We are grateful to them and to a far-sighted Steering Committee.

In this volume the authors present the results of field investigations into the operational strategy of construction firms and relate it to the theoretical analysis in the companion volume. The major conclusions come as no real surprise to me. There is a gap between theory and practice. If it is to be bridged, real effort is required on the part of both academics and managers.

At the start of the SPP I reported to SERC that there existed a problem of information transfer. Over a period of some thirty years many papers had been written which were pertinent to managers in the construction industry. They had never been discussed seriously within the industry itself. There were, and still are, many reasons for this failure but we can highlight two.

First, academics write for their peers and for the further development of their own discipline and the pressure to do this is increasing. Few of the journals in which they publish are found on the desks of the captains of industry. Second, if theoretical ideas are brought before the leaders of industry they do not often meet with a response. There are still very few in construction firms who have been trained to apply research findings relevant to management.

The situation is now changing as a result of economic and technological pressures. Academics are more willing (and even in some cases more able) to target a non-specialist audience and to try to demonstrate the practical application of their research. Industrialists are becoming increasingly aware of the growing need to ensure that their staff have the requisite knowledge to operate efficiently in an internationally competitive environment and hence of the importance of continuing education.

Progress has been slow – but the pace is quickening and it is my hope that the present work will not only serve to show where the gaps are but will also lead to a dialogue to determine how they may be bridged.

I believe that both this book and the companion volume are of relevance to academics and to managers in the construction industry as well as to those who are closely involved with the industry including students of construction disciplines, some of whom will be the leaders of tomorrow.

Pat Hillebrandt and Jacquie Cannon have done a splendid job though they, I am sure, would agree that it is only a start. They have, however, given a very clear set of sailing directions and I am grateful to them for doing so and for letting me be involved in drawing them up.

W.D. BIGGS

Acknowledgements

Our thanks go first to the many members of the construction firms who took part in the research and who gave so generously of their time to discuss the operations of their firms and their particular role in it. Their willingness to participate in the project and their cooperation were much appreciated. We should like to record our thanks to them all, including the firms listed below who have permitted us to refer to them by name: AMEC plc; Balfour Beatty Ltd; Henry Boot & Sons plc; Bovis Ltd; Cementation Ltd; Costain Group plc; Robert M. Douglas Holdings plc; Galliford plc; Haden Young; Higgs & Hill plc; John Laing plc; Y.J. Lovell Holdings plc; Alfred McAlpine plc; John Mowlem & Co. plc; Nortwest Holst Holdings plc; Shepherd Construction Ltd; Tarmac plc; Taylor Woodrow plc.

We wish to express our appreciation to friends, colleagues and family for helpful support and comment at all stages of the project and in particular to Sir Peter Trench who gave much wise counsel in the early stages of the project. Most important of all our gratitude is to Bill Biggs who guided, cajoled and supported us so cheerfully and valiantly through the whole process of the study. The book would not have been possible without the willing help of Sheila Rogers, the Secretary of the Department of Construction Management at the University of Reading, and her team. We thank them all.

PATRICIA M. HILLEBRANDT
JACQUELINE CANNON

Abbreviations and Acronyms

BEC	Building Employers Confederation
CBI	Confederation of British Industry
CIOB	Chartered Institute of Building
CITB	Construction Industry Training Board
DoE	Department of the Environment
ECGD	Export Credits Guarantee Department
EDC	Economic Development Committee
FCEC	Federation of Civil Engineering Contractors
FDI	Foreign direct investment
HMSO	Her Majesty's Stationery Office
HNC	Higher National Certificate
ILM	Internal labour market
INSEAD	European Institute of Business Administration
JCT	Joint Contracts Tribunal
NEDO	National Economic Development Office
ONC	Ordinary National Certificate
OPCS	Office of Population Census and Surveys
SERC	Science and Engineering Research Council
SGB	Scaffolding Great Britain plc
SPP	Specially Promoted Programme (for research in construction management)
UNDP	United Nations Development Programme
USAID	United States Agency for International Development

Introduction

1 THE PROJECT

This book represents the second half of a project on the strategic behaviour of large UK building and civil engineering firms, all with some overseas experience. The project originated because it was thought that the way in which large construction firms operate had been largely neglected by researchers. There was a need to link relevant aspects of economics, management, sociological and financial theories in investigating the way those large firms function and to examine how relevant those theories seemed to be to the specific characteristics and behaviour of construction firms.

The first half of the project offers a number of theoretical approaches from different disciplines which help to analyse and explain the decision-making processes of large construction firms. It is published as the companion volume to this one and is entitled *The Management of Construction Firms: Aspects of Theory*. The second part of the project consisted of a series of interviews with the principal decision-makers in about twenty of the largest UK construction firms. The contents of the discussions are the subject of this volume. The project was undertaken at the University of Reading and funded by the SERC Specially Promoted Programme in Construction Management.

The purpose of the interviews was to investigate how construction firms take their strategic decisions; to assess the relevance of the aspects of theory discussed in the companion book to the behaviour of large construction firms and the extent to which the firms' strategies were implicitly or explicitly related to those aspects of theory.

The interviews took the form of discussions rather than formal question-and-answer sessions. The total number of firms asked to participate in the project was twenty-six, and twenty of these agreed in principle. The twenty-six approached included all the top twenty contractors reckoned by turnover (though not any that were mainly housebuilders). Of these top twenty, fourteen agreed to cooperate. The remaining six contractors approached were chosen because they were among the thirty-five largest companies, because of their international connections or because the researchers wished to explore in greater detail some particular area of operations of the industry. All six agreed to participate in the project. Those who refused to participate did so either because they did not cooperate in research projects of this type, or for some special and understandable reason they could not devote time to the project but would have done so in different circumstances.

It is estimated that the twenty contractors who agreed to cooperate in the project accounted for about 12 per cent of the new work done by contractors in the United Kingdom and about 60 per cent of the contracting work by the top thirty-five companies.

In most cases interviews were conducted with main board members closely connected with contracting activities (as distinct from housing, property development or other operations) or senior non-board executives. Not every aspect of the company's activities was covered in equal detail over the whole range of companies. Since the overall objective was to understand how construction firms as a whole behave, it was sometimes necessary to devote a considerable proportion of the time spent with a certain company on a particular aspect of its operation, for example, a takeover situation, a change in internal structure or a change in the relationship of part of the company to the whole, to its subsidiaries or to a parent company.

All quotations are anonymous as all those who took part in the interviews were given the authors' assurances that their identity would not be revealed, though one or two permitted statements which could identify them.

2 THE CONTENT OF THE BOOK

In order to understand how and for what reasons the large companies have adopted particular strategies in the 1980s, it is necessary to set the scene by establishing the major external and internal events which have affected the construction industry and its development since the early 1970s. This is one of the functions of Chapter 1. The other is to set in context the large firms of the industry.

The overall strategy and objectives of the companies which were interviewed are described and discussed in Chapter 2. This is followed by Chapter 3 on growth and diversification which involve strategic decisions both by construction firms and by those acquiring construction firms.

Chapter 4 deals with financial policy and highlights the way in which contracting differs from other construction activities including manufacturing. The following chapter focuses on marketing and bidding policy, mainly for work in the United Kingdom because Chapter 6 deals with all aspects of international policy.

The diversity in the structure and organisation of the companies is the subject of Chapter 7. The next two chapters deal with human resources of the construction firms: Chapter 8 deals with the management policies and Chapter 9 with the way labour is employed – by direct employment or by subcontracting.

Finally Chapter 10 draws together the evidence from the interviews and relates the main findings to the relevant theoretical concepts developed in the companion book. It also suggests how the industry's performance could be enhanced by closer acquaintance with the ideas and analysis developed by researchers and the areas where further research would benefit the industry.

Part I
Background

1 The Industry Yesterday and Today

1.1 STRUCTURE OF THE INDUSTRY AND THE LARGE FIRMS

In spite of the many changes which have affected the construction industry in the past two decades its structure has remained largely unaltered, with a small number of very large firms and a vast number of small firms swollen recently by the move towards self-employment. In 1987 the thirty-five large firms employing more than 1200 persons accounted for 18 per cent of the new workload compared with 134 000 firms employing 1–3 persons (i.e. not including self-employed) with 9 per cent of the workload of the industry.[1] Table 1.1 shows in more detail the distribution of the work done, analysed by the size of firm (measured by numbers employed) as well as by the number of firms involved. The firms which took part in the interviews probably accounted for nearly two-thirds of the work done by the largest category of firms, or say £2500 million of work. Their total turnover was much greater than this because of all their other activities.

It is possible to obtain more data on the size and range of activities of large firms from annual accounts and other published data. Table 1.2 shows construction companies with turnover in excess of £100 million which include building and civil engineering in their work. Among these very large firms there are some with activities either upstream and/or downstream from contracting – for example, materials – or with quite different activities. Some of these are shown in Table 1.3.

In the past ten years there have been a number of mergers and takeovers affecting the largest construction companies. For example, BICC has taken over Haden Young, Beazer has been on the take-over path for a number of years and has swallowed French Kier among others. AMEC was formed by a merger of William Press and Leonard Fairclough and has recently taken over Matthew Hall. Mowlem has merged with SGB. Although the ranking of some of those large companies in terms of turnover may have changed in the

3

Table 1.1 Number of firms and value of work done in 1987, analysed by size of firm

Size of firm (classified by numbers of employed)[a]	Number of firms	Value of work done (£million current prices)[b]
1200 and over	35	3 675
600–1199	71	2 369
100–599	143	2 309
115–299	507	3 405
80–114	393	1 299
60–79	456	1 121
35–59	1 520	2 327
25–34	1 507	1 371
14–24	4 485	2 472
8–13	7 074	1 948
4–7	24 838	2 977
2–3	54 712	2 794
1	79 354	2 111
Total[c]	175 095	30 172

Notes: (a) See note 1. These figures exclude the self-employed.
(b) Based on four times the third-quarter figures.
(c) Individual figures may not sum to total because of roundings.
Source: Department of the Environment, *Housing and Construction Statistics 1977–87* (London: HMSO, 1988) Tables 3.3 and 3.7.

past decades those who were at the top thirty years ago still appear as important in Table 1.2.

The ownership of the large companies is unusual inasmuch as about a quarter are family-controlled. The same proportion of family controlled firms were interviewed in this study. Another quarter had strong family connections in their management.

1.2 WORKLOAD FLUCTUATIONS

The near-continuous boom enjoyed by the construction industry from the early 1950s came to an abrupt halt with the first oil crisis of 1973. Fluctuations in the level of construction activity did occur during that period and the members of the construction industry made numerous representations to government about the adverse impact of stops and goes on the well-being of construction firms. In

Table 1.2 Thirty-five construction companies with turnover in excess of £100 million in years 1986 to 1988 (£million current prices)

Company	Year end	Turnover 1986	1987	1988
AMEC[1]	Dec	711	794	1310
Balfour Beatty[2]	Dec	988	1187	1359
Beazer	June	507	1033	1343
Biwater	Dec	124	136	183
Boot (Henry)	Dec	160	153	170
Bovis[3]	Dec	630	856	1116
Bryant Group	May	157	201	260
Budge (A.F.)	Dec	71	92	140
Conder	Dec	123	125	128
Costain	Dec	740	880	1083
Crest Nicholson	Oct	212	223	268
Douglas Holdings (R.M.)	March	146	143	182
Egerton Trust	Dec	75	114	111
Galliford	June	108	134	169
Gleeson Group (M.J.)	June	92	109	109
Higgs & Hill	Dec	239	267	343
Laing (John)	Dec	864	1064	1350
Lawrence (Walter)	Dec	177	207	238
Lilley (F.J.C.)	Jan	331	257	204
Lovell Holdings (Y.J.)	Sept	267	324	383
McAlpine (Alfred)	Oct	483	583	591
Miller Group	Dec	127	187	234
Monk & Company (A)	Mar	136	131	178
Mowlem (John)	Dec	636	793	991
Newarthill (Sir Robert McAlpine)	Oct	273	343	416
Norwest Holst	March	230	208	253
Rush & Tompkins	March	184	217	217
Shepherd Construction	June	155	187	239
Tarmac	Dec	1735	2201	2840
Taylor Woodrow	Dec	793	902	1260
Tilbury Group	Dec	108	140	184
Trafalgar House	Sept	2071	2368	2676
Wates Building Group	Dec	166	209	237
Wiltshier Group (John)	Dec	141	144	181
Wimpey	Dec	1461	1482	1730

Notes: [1]AMEC acquired Matthew Hall in 1988.
[2]Balfour Beatty is a subsidiary of BICC plc.
[3]Bovis is a subsidiary of P & O plc.

the context of a managed economy and given the nature of the industry, stops and goes were unavoidable.

Table 1.3 Diversification by selected construction companies

Company	Building civil engineering	House building	Property Development	Mining Offshore	Aggregates etc.	Other Building materials	Plant	Mechanical Electrical Engineering	Builders Merchants Wholesalers	Other
AMEC	✓	✓	✓	✓				✓		
Beazer	✓	✓	✓			✓				
Bryant Group	✓	✓	✓							Time share
Costain	✓		✓	✓	✓					Time share, Form work
Douglas Holdings	✓		✓	✓	✓		✓			Health care
Egerton Trust	✓	✓	✓	✓			✓			
Galliford	✓	✓	✓				✓		✓	
Higgs & Hill	✓	✓	✓				✓			
Laing (John)	✓	✓	✓				✓			
Lovell Holdings	✓	✓	✓				✓	✓		Stolport,
Mowlem (John)	✓	✓	✓				✓			Equipment instruments
Tarmac	✓	✓	✓		✓	✓		✓		Ford main dealer,
Taylor Woodrow	✓	✓	✓	✓	✓		✓			Printing, Waste disposal
Wimpey	✓	✓	✓	✓	✓		✓			Consultancy

From 1955 – when the last controls on construction had been removed – to 1973, the total workload of the industry doubled. Between 1973 and 1981, the industry's output fell by about 22 per cent which brought it back to the level of the early 1960s. It is not expected to reach the peak in the level of activity of 1973 until 1988.[2]

The mix of output of the industry has also changed, especially since 1973. In particular public sector new housing and other public sector new work have declined substantially and commercial building has increased dramatically. In the same period private housing and industrial building have fluctuated.

In the middle of the 1950s, the output on repair and maintenance was about 25 per cent of total workload. Its share rose fairly steadily in the 1960s onwards to reach over 30 per cent in 1976,[3] over 40 per cent in 1980 and to a peak of 46 per cent in 1985 since when it has fallen back a little.[4]

Since official statistics do not take into account repair and maintenance work undertaken by some private organisations or public sector bodies, and make no allowance for the activities of the black economy, the total amount of repair and maintenance work is estimated to be well over the official total. On the basis that DoE data collection may miss some output, it has been suggested that total repair and maintenance work may account for well over 50 per cent of the level of activity in construction and may even be near 60 per cent.

Large contracting firms which concentrate their operations on new work have therefore not shared in the growth of repair and maintenance. Moreover, in the last decade, contraction of public housing programmes has considerably reduced their role in the sector.

If the contribution of repair and maintenance work to total output is excluded, and public housebuilding activity is likewise deducted from new work on the ground that the small size of individual projects makes them unattractive to large contractors, the total workload in which large firms have shared has increased by 33 per cent since 1981, from £11 925 million to £16 126 million in 1987 (1985 prices).[5] It is still 12 per cent below the workload of 1973.

The bulk of the increase in the level of activity in the past few years has been concentrated in the commercial sector. Office development in London and the south-east has been the dominant source of the recent expansion in new work. In 1987, the south-east of the country generated 84 per cent of the total value of orders for offices, 50 per cent of all other commercial orders and 63 per cent of industrial orders.[6]

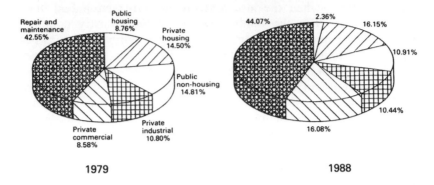

Figure 1.1 Construction output by sector £million (1985 prices)

The worst falls faced by large contractors in the 1980s occurred in civil engineering, as a result of cutbacks in the level of expenditure by the public sector. In order to retain their share in a shrinking market, contractors with civil engineering divisions pared tender prices so that the index for all road construction contracts (1985=100) fell from 98 in 1980 to 90 in 1981 and did not exceed 98 again until 1985.[7] At the same time, they made efforts to move into new building sectors, such as private housing and also made strenuous attempts to replace infrastructure work (which was no longer available from the public sector) by privately funded projects.

Figure 1.1 shows the output for the main sectors of construction in 1979 and 1988. There has also been a dramatic change in the size of contracts as is shown by Table 1.4.

The fall in the number of public new housing large contracts is even more marked than the fall in the total value of public housing orders for contractors, while the value of large contracts in the private housing sector has fallen in spite of the increase in contractors' new orders overall.

In non-housing work the value of large contracts in both the public sector and the private industrial sector have fallen along with a small fall of orders for contractors in real terms over the period. The startling change is in private commercial work where the value of large contracts has increased nearly threefold while the number of orders received by contractors has rather more than doubled in real terms. The total value of the work available to contractors in large contracts has fallen slightly (4 per cent) between 1977 and 1986. Over this same period the number of contracts over £2 million increased by

Table 1.4 Estimated value of new orders of over £2m (1986 prices) received by contractors in 1977 and 1986.

	Value of orders over £2m (1986 prices)		Number	
	1977	*1986*	*1977*	*1986*
New housing				
Public	1118	106	299	157
Private	122	101	30	38
Other new work				
Public	2256	1812	348	333
Private industrial	720	612	128	163
Private commercial	722	2115	115	377
Total new work	4938	4746	920	1068

Note: Prices from 1977 to 1986 approximately doubled. It follows that orders over £2M in 1986 were equivalent to orders over £1M in 1977. Thus the 1977 column is orders over £1 million at 1977 prices, converted to orders over £2m at 1986 prices.

Sources: DoE, *Housing and Construction Statistics 1970–1980* (London: HMSO, 1981) Table 7(a), and DoE, *Housing and Construction Statistics 1976–1986 (HMSO)* (London: HMSO, 1987) Tables A and 1.4(d).

16 per cent. It has been estimated that the number of large contracts fell in the period 1971 to 1981 so that the increase must have taken place since 1981.[8]

In addition, large UK contractors, which shared fully in the boom with other international construction firms in the Middle East, have seen the total value of work available overseas fall very sharply and work undertaken overseas has fallen from £2324 million (current prices) for the financial year 1982/3 down to £1696 million in the calendar year 1987. The fall in constant prices is obviously considerably greater and the volume of work in 1987 would be substantially less than in 1982/3.[9]

1.3 TECHNOLOGY

Fluctuations in total output and in its mix have been accompanied by many changes in the use of resources – both manpower and building products – and in their management.

Pressure of demand in the 1960s and early 1970s, together with the requirements for public sector clients to select lowest tenders, combined to favour the adoption of system building, based largely on heavy industrialised methods, for many public housing and other public projects. The same technology was used, though to a lesser extent, in some of the commercial developments of that period. Reliance on systems which had been inadequately tested has proved costly. Vandalism, low occupancy rates and rejection by public housing tenants have in some cases led to demolition, in others to expensive refurbishment programmes. Rapid obsolescence of offices built during those years has been partly responsible for the growth of rehabilitation programmes.

In recent years the building services element in building projects has grown rapidly and the relevant technology developed faster than that of the building itself. The reasons for this are twofold. On the one hand, there have been rapid developments in the control of the environment within buildings. On the other, the rapid adoption of information technology has had a major impact on the integration of services within new offices and shops in particular. It has also considerably boosted the number and value of renovation programmes. The increased importance of the services element has reinforced the shift away from direct employment and towards specialist subcontracting.

1.4   SUBCONTRACTING

This shift has three components. First, there has been a move towards more use of supply-and-fix contractors – that is, those who supply both labour and materials – for example, for heating and ventilating and electrical work, which are becoming increasingly important in new large industrial and commercial buildings. Second, there is an increase in labour-only subcontracting which has been in existence a long time,[10] but was boosted by the brief existence of selective employment tax in the mid-1960s. It has continued to develop so that in the south of England far fewer persons are now employed directly by large main contractors and most of the labour force has self-employed status. In the north of the country the practice is still spreading. Third, there has been a change in contractual arrangements so that with more management contracting even large contractors may themselves be subcontractors.

The merits and demerits of some of these changes and the reasons for them are mentioned elsewhere in this book. Suffice it to mention some of the major effects: breakdown in the traditional training arrangements so that there are both insufficient training in the industry and insufficient attempts to match training to skills required; a decrease in the requirements for working capital and greater flexibility of contractors to work anywhere in the country without having to transfer their labour force or recruit their own in the areas concerned. *En passant* it is worth remarking, however, that when those in the industry lament the rise of labour-only subcontracting they tend to relate it to operatives permanently employed by contractors, whereas in fact it largely replaces the system of casual employment which was already the lament of some concerned with the industry even in the 1960s.

One of the consequences of these changes is that there is no satisfactory measure of the size of firms in the industry since neither numbers employed nor turnover necessarily represent the amount of work actually carried out.

1.5 CHANGES IN THE PROCESS

The increase in management contracting is but part of a move towards a greater variety of ways of organising the process of construction including the roles assumed by contractors: of *designers* in design and build (D&B) or design and construct (D&C) where they may either use their own in-house design staff or contract with an architect or engineer to undertake the design; of *managers* on behalf of the client of the whole process of procurement of buildings or works or of the construction part of it alone, of *principals* in putting together a project including finance, design, construction and often commissioning and management of the finished project.

One of the consequences of many of these changes is that the contractor is moving closer to the client who is himself becoming more sophisticated and is often now the driving force for improvements in the construction process. This is partly the consequence of the increased concentration of large sectors of industry. Ramsay's view that 'the agent for change . . . is not likely to be the client'[11] is not borne out by developments over the past few years.

1.6 THE ROLE OF GOVERNMENT

The reduction in the amount of work for the public sector in house-building and civil engineering has already been noted. The infrastructural needs of the country ensured a considerable role for the public sector as client of the industry in the two decades up to the early 1970s. The total of the industry's activity in new work on behalf of the public sector reached £9425 million (at 1985 prices) in 1973 when it represented 44 per cent of all new work. By 1987, new work on behalf of the public sector had dropped to £4469 million at 1985 prices, which represented 26 per cent of total new work.[12]

While the public sector held the prime place as client of the industry, the government also exerted a profound influence as guardian and setter of standards of performance and as sponsor of the bulk of the research and development activity undertaken for the industry. The sponsor role of the relevant departments or ministries within government was a major responsibility and the Group of Eight, which brought together construction employers, employees and professional organisations saw as its main function that of pressure group, especially when stops loomed on the horizon. The rundown of public sector work has a number of reasons:

1. The policy of privatisation of public assets, which has been one of the major policy planks in the past decade, has permanently shifted construction work previously carried out on behalf of some nationalised industry or local authority to the private sector. The work is still there. It simply appears under a different heading.
2. Those industries which are still in the public sector, some for the time being only, have had their capital programmes rigidly controlled by the Treasury.
3. Local authorities have come under increasingly tight financial control by the central government and their spending power has been severely curbed though 'creative' accounting measures may have kept spending higher than it might otherwise have been. At the same time, they have had to allocate a rising share of available resources to the rehabilitation of rundown, neglected or defective housing estates.
4. The real value of other programmes has been cut back either to fit in with the requirements of fiscal policy or as the inevitable outcome of demographic changes as in the education sector, for instance.

As the public sector's profound and widespread influence on the construction industry waned, failure by private sector organisations to pick up the mantle thus set aside led to a growing gap in policy-making in the industry. The Building and Civil Engineering Economic Development Committees (EDCs), which might have provided an alternative source of influence, were thwarted in their attempts by the failure of some employers' and employees' associations to develop new attitudes and enthusiasm to replace the interventionist role of government.

The industry itself was unable to convince the Treasury that private infrastructure projects would not run counter to government policy as embodied in the Medium Term Financial Strategy. Training policy has been largely neglected as the bureaucratic structure of the training agencies has prevented an adequate response to the rapidly changing requirements of the industry. In a number of areas a smaller public role has left a gap which has not yet been filled by private endeavours.

NOTES AND REFERENCES

1. These figures are those available from Department of the Environment (DoE) *Housing and Construction Statistics 1977–87* (London: HMSO, 1988) Tables 3.10 and 3.14. Because of the large and varying number of self-employed persons used by contractors who would formerly have employed their own labour directly, the groups classified by numbers employed are no longer a good indication of the total work done by a firm. It is possible for a firm with a large turnover to subcontract almost all its work so that in the statistics it would appear to be employing relatively few people. Nevertheless the firms interviewed in this project would almost certainly all be employing over 1200 persons.
2. Joint Forecasting Committee for the Construction Industries, *Construction Forecasts 1988–1989–1990* (London: NEDO, 1988).
3. DoE, *Housing and Construction Statistics*, various issues.
4. DoE, *Housing and Construction Statistics 1977–87* (London: HMSO, 1988) Table 1.6.
5. DoE, as note 3, and note 4, Table 1.7.
6. DoE, as note 4, Table 1.3.
7. DoE, as note 4, Table A.
8. Hillebrandt, Patricia M., *Analysis of the British Construction Industry* (London: Macmillan, 1984) p. 83, Table 4.6.
9. DoE, as note 4, Table 1.11.
10. *Report of the Committee of Inquiry under Professor E.H. Phelps Brown into certain Matters concerning Labour in Building and Civil Engineering* (London: HMSO, 1968) Cmnd. 3714.

11. Ramsay, W., 'Business Objectives and Strategy' in Hillebrandt, P.M. and Cannon, J., *The Management of Construction Firms: Aspects of Theory* (London: Macmillan, 1989) p. 26.
12. DoE, as note 3.

Part II
Overall Strategy of Large Firms

2 Objectives and Strategy of Firms

2.1 INTRODUCTION

Writing on 'Business Objectives and Strategy' in the companion volume, Ramsay distinguishes the mission of the firm, the objectives and the strategy.[1]

One of the problems about these three concepts is that, both in writings on theory and in practical use, objectives, strategy and planning are used in an ill-defined way, their meaning varying according to the person using the terms. In order to be able to relate the statements made during the interviews to a common framework, the definitions adopted in this chapter for mission, objective, strategy and planning, given below, follow closely those adopted by Ramsay: 'The mission (or vision) of a business is its long-term ambition, what it ideally wants to become over time. This is usually expressed in qualitative terms and is probably never achieved exactly or totally' (p. 10).

Objectives are finite in time, shorter term than mission, quantitative and precede strategy. The time-frame is important and usually extends up to five years. *Strategy* does not include objectives. It is about the *means* of meeting these objectives. It needs to be formulated in such a way that those responsible for implementing it are clear as to what they have to achieve, and that progress can be easily assessed. As Ramsay put it, 'The management of the firm should be committed to the objectives of the business. There is obviously no point in developing a strategy to meet certain objectives if there is no commitment to them in the first place' (p. 11).

Strategic planning is the process by which strategy is agreed or defined. *Planning* is the formalised process by which the agreed strategy is translated into more detailed targets and required action within a time-frame. It will normally extend to a period not exceeding three years and in the very short term of six months to one year, it includes budgeting.

In the companies interviewed, there is generally a blurred line between mission and objectives and further blurred lines between

17

objectives, strategy and planning. In a number of companies, there is a concept of mission though it is often called objective, such as 'to be a truly national and international contractor'; 'to achieve excellence in quality of performance and profit'. With the exception of very few companies, objectives are imprecise and lack a time-frame which prevents the development of a coherent strategy. There is thus often a missing link between objectives and planning.

Objectives and strategy do not always require action at levels below that of the board of a company. It is possible for an objective to be met by the actions of a single member of the board. The purchase of a company in the USA may be masterminded by the managing director. He will have implicitly translated the board's objective into a strategy and hence a plan without having need to communicate this to other levels of management.

A number of objectives require action over a period of time by several levels of management within the company and in this situation it is very important that they should be translated into strategic terms and detailed operational plans which are fully communicated to all those involved. In some companies, this process works well and is carefully tailored to ensure that the board can monitor progress towards targets as well as deviations from targets which require swift remedial action. In others, the objectives and the strategy, where they exist, are neither properly disseminated nor turned into plans for action by those who should be involved. There are even cases where the board is not fully aware of the objectives which the subsidiaries have set themselves.

2.2 MISSION AND OBJECTIVES

Because of the difficulty of separating mission and objectives during the company interviews, they are here dealt with together. They may be divided into three broad categories: (i) financial; (ii) quality of performance or relationships, and (iii) size and type of business. There are differences in emphasis in these between the companies which are part of a conglomerate, those which have strong family control or connections, and those which are neither of these. In the companies which are part of a conglomerate the maximisation of profit or cash flow is dominant. They are set financial targets by the group board and it is these targets which heavily influence their strategies. Quality, though important to all the companies, is secondary and a means to the financial ends. The type of business is largely dictated by the holding company. If the holding company already has other subsidiaries in a particular activity related to construction – for example, property development, housing or plant and equipment – the contracting subsidiary is precluded from engaging in any of those businesses. As these businesses have been a logical development for a number of contracting firms (see Chapter 3) the contractors in the conglomerates are deprived of some sources of growth and profitability.

The family firms generally have a wide range of objectives and, with one or two exceptions, the word 'maximise' was rarely used in the interviews. The emphasis is on a proper balance between financial objectives, such as an *acceptable* return on shareholders' assets, profitable growth, or the reduction of gearing, and more social objectives related to honesty, good relationships with the workforce, reputation, as well as in some cases growth, modernisation of the company and development of new areas of activity. In a few cases of past difficulties the current objective is simply to reinstate the earlier profitable situation. The family firms are in theory free to enter any type of business but in practice are hindered by their inability to raise capital without diluting the family shareholdings, thus restricting growth.

The remaining companies vary in their approach with the whole range of objectives being represented, generally with more stress on finance and profitable growth than in the family firms. They have the widest choice in the selection of the markets or businesses they wish to enter. In the limited information on management buy-outs the means of survival for the company takes absolute priority. This implies improving financial performance and consideration of the several ways to achieve this objective including whether to merge with a company of their choice or to remain independent.

In all companies, some of the objectives have changed over time. Indeed, because of the stresses and strains of the change in the construction markets outlined in Chapter 1 the firms have been forced over the past ten years or so to rethink their objectives and many of these have already been achieved so that their present objectives are sometimes those of continuing expansion of their existing markets rather than major restructuring of their previous range of activities.

In a number of companies, the broadening of the contractor's role to one of acting as the principal in the initiation of projects is now being elevated to that of a major formal objective, with increasing importance for their future well-being. The switch in those companies has important consequences for their strategies, particularly in terms of the necessary senior management skills required to implement the relevant strategies.

A few companies have not developed any formal set of coherent objectives and at the time of the research were suffering from this deficiency and attempting to formulate them.

2.3   OBJECTIVES AND STRATEGY

It may be useful to analyse the discussion on strategy along the lines suggested by Ramsay and following Ansoff,[2] that is, scope, resource allocation, competitive advantage and synergy.

In some of the construction companies visited strategy was equated with planning and planning sometimes tended to be short-term and related to financial budgeting and forward planning. Yet when questions were asked about strategy most people were able to talk enthusiastically and cogently about it in spite of its not always being formally discussed or accepted within the firm.

Other contractors have a very clear written strategy and regularly revise it to deal with changing circumstances. Relevant elements of it are communicated to and discussed with those concerned with its implementation. In those companies it is noteworthy that strategy is formulated from the top down as well as from the bottom up. There are many companies with strategic approaches which fitted between these two extremes.

2.3.1   Scope

The scope of a construction business is the first and arguably the most important strategic question. Its extent and its limits may be considered at two levels: (i) the overall scope in large corporations which have a number of different activities; and (ii) the scope of a business which has mainly contracting operations. The former is largely dealt with in Chapter 3 on growth and diversification. The latter is considered here in Ramsay's terms (pp. 11–12) of '*who* is being satisfied' – the type of client; '*what* is being satisfied' – the types of demand; and '*how* are these needs being satisfied' – dealt with here in terms of the geographical area of operations and the way in which the contracting business meets demand.

The construction industry is unusual in the sense that its clients fall into two entirely different categories, public sector and private sector. In companies with a long history of undertaking public sector work, mainly in civil engineering, reference was made to the particular skills which they had developed in dealing with public sector clients but, in all companies visited, it is the level and type of work which matters and not the identity of the client.

In general the contractors interviewed are prepared to undertake any type of building or civil engineering work. There are, however, some exceptions:

1. No contractor will undertake small contracts except where he is obliging an existing client. The reason is that the overhead costs of managing small contracts are disproportionate to their total value. This is the explanation for their not undertaking repair and maintenance work but being willing to bid for large renovation schemes.
2. At the other end of the scale, there is a limit to the size of project which they will handle on their own. This is a function of risk on one contract relative to the total workload of the company. Joint ventures are the answer to this type of problem.
3. Some firms do not have the skills required to undertake very large projects of a very specialised nature and which occur infrequently such as nuclear-power stations, oil platforms or refineries.
4. A few firms are specialists in a particular type of work either in their main operations or as specialist subcontractors in a particular field.
5. A few companies have now effectively withdrawn from overseas work.
6. All contractors wish for a broad and balanced range of activities since it enables them to take advantage of growth in a particular sector of the market and restricts their exposure to risk in any one of them.

Most of the companies interviewed have a spread of activity over the whole of the UK, but one in particular has had some problems in changing its public image from that of a regional company to a national company even after it had set up a good regional network.

Almost all of them operate from some regional office network as described in Chapter 7.

All companies have had some operations abroad and most are still in overseas markets but they have needed to use their strategic planning mechanisms to consider what to do after the fall in the very lucrative markets of the Middle East. In one case in particular the long-term buoyant Middle East market provided the time and opportunity for major long-term planning and enabled the company to strengthen its financial asset base and to use it as a springboard for diversification.

Because contractors do not normally undertake the design or manufacture of components, they do not carry out their own design or product research and development from which they would otherwise obtain strong competitive advantage. In contracting the design is normally undertaken elsewhere and the contractor has limited ability to differentiate his product from those of other contractors on technical merit. However, there are other ways in which the contractor can offer the client a service such as shorter contract duration, quality of work and good client–contractor relationships. Moreover the contractor can offer a variety of services which are different from the traditional contracting service. These include design and build, management contracting, project management, financial packages, equipping and furnishing the building, maintenance contracts, and management of the facilities. All contractors offer some of these services. Very few of them analyse their positions in these markets in a logical way. One method of doing this is the growth-share matrix developed by the Boston Consulting Group to enable companies to evaluate the various products of business units in their portfolios. This is discussed in more detail by Ramsay in the companion volume (Chapter 2). Basically it relates and compares on a matrix the rate of growth of markets, market share relative to the leading competitor and the sales revenue from each market.

It enables markets to be classified as:

1. 'stars' which are high-growth, high-market-share businesses but which probably use as much cash as they generate;
2. problem businesses which are high-growth markets where the company is *not* a market leader but which need a lot of cash;
3. 'cash cows' that is businesses where the growth in the market is low but the company has a high share so it generates cash;
4. the 'dogs' of the company, that is, low-growth and low-market-

share businesses which use up whatever cash they generate just to keep going.

Ramsay comments that:

> The share-growth matrix is a simple one-shot analysis which can suggest ways of allocating resources within the company. Strategic decisions as to whether to invest, hold, harvest or divest can be suggested for different products or services in the company's portfolio.[3] Its apparent simplicity, however, should not disguise the fact that it is much more complicated than it looks. Just to define the market to which the product or service belongs can be fraught with difficulty. Many market definitions are either too large or too small to be meaningful (p. 16).

One person interviewed who was put in charge of marketing had been able to consider his market in an orderly fashion with the help of this matrix (see Chapter 5). This was rare.

There are other ways of thinking about the strategy for various businesses which are discussed by Ramsay, including some which bring in greater judgement especially about the future and the way competitors may behave.

Unlike companies where scope is limited by the capacity and supply of fixed assets, this was not a barrier mentioned by any of the companies visited. This makes plain why flexibility was seen as a major advantage. 'A construction firm needs above all to be flexible and to shift markets if necessary.' In fact scope was limited by the availability of opportunities for growth and by the managerial capacity.

2.3.2 Resource allocation

The principal resource of construction companies is management. The deployment of management is fundamental to the efficient operation of the business and is largely dictated by decisions on scope. All contractors stress the importance of management as a resource. Ramsay said that 'if the firm really believes . . . that people are its most important attribute and the factor that distinguishes it from its competition it will act accordingly and spell it out in "its strategy"' (p. 12). They do believe it but they rarely spell it out in their strategy.

The allocation of managers is very different in construction from other industries because it is project-based and therefore short-term and finite. There is therefore a constant juggling of site managers between projects. Most firms expressed a preference for obtaining as large a proportion of their senior managers as possible from within the organisation. The movement of managers from one project to another is therefore not only a requirement for proper training but also necessary because of the need to man new projects as they come on stream. This mobility and isolation from head office together with the employment of subcontractors calls for a strong identification of the manager with the company's general philosophy and name as well as its approach to the management of sites. Only thus is efficient transfer of managerial skills possible. It also means that it takes some time for new recruits to the company at senior site-management level to be tested and become good company men. This factor limits the growth rate of the company because it limits the rate at which new managers can be absorbed. All companies stressed the importance of a permanent continuing management cohort but it did happen that managers were engaged purely to work on one project.

The allocation of other manpower is first a question of whether to subcontract or to have a directly employed labour force. This is discussed in Chapter 9. Second, the allocation of directly employed manpower will depend on the needs of the various projects.

Because the fixed assets in construction at site level are confined to plant and temporary buildings both of which can be hired rather than owned, there is little to say on this aspect of resource allocation. Indeed the ownership of plant is one aspect of diversification policy which is covered in Chapter 3. There is also little to say about the allocation of funds on the contracting side of construction because it is a cash-generating activity.

2.3.3 Competitive advantage

According to Ramsay there are effectively 'only two basic strategies [to secure a substantial advantage against competitors]: one based on cost, the other on differentiation' (p. 19).

The competitive advantage of contracting firms cannot be linked to a standard product as in manufacturing industry because there is no standard product.

The traditional method of contracting with selective tender limits product differentiation. Differentiation is possible only until selection has taken place; thereafter competition is on price alone. Open competition does not even allow this degree of product differentiation because the tender price is the only criterion adopted. These systems were *de rigueur* in the public sector and selective tendering was widely used in the post-war years in the private sector. This narrow interpretation of competition purely on price gradually broke down first in the private and more recently in the public sector. There is now a whole range of arrangements for the selection of contractors which permit the contractor to include other services and thus to differentiate his products. This is one way in which the contractor can increase his control over his business.

There are four distinct ways of differentiating the product, some of which may be used together:

(i) by offering a range of different ways of managing the project;
(ii) by the extension of the construction phase backwards into design;
(iii) by the extension of the traditional project backwards beyond the construction phase to include putting together a financial package;
(iv) by the forward extension to include equipping and furnishing the building, maintenance of the building or structure and the management of the facility.

Most contractors offer the first two, many are concerned to increase their involvement in financial packages, and several are prepared to undertake the fourth but have not yet acquired a reputation for doing so. In some cases companies have gone into the first two, that is, design and construct and some form of management contracting to meet the requirements of specific clients and find themselves undertaking a considerable amount of work that they did not originally perceive to be a major market area. Indeed growth in design and build or in some other non-traditional organisation of the process will normally be at the expense of work along traditional lines. All contractors are keen to differentiate the product if it is considered that this would in any way reduce uncertainty about the level of workload beyond that of existing contracts. Hence contractors are generally willing to undertake any form of non-traditional contract and are fully aware of the respective advantages and disadvantages of various types of arrangement. In particular, they lose the advantage of a positive cash flow where finance does not go through their hands. Second, if payment is by fee they lose the opportunity for large profits in exchange for less risk of loss. Third, if the profit element is small, it may be a waste of management resource which could perhaps earn a higher profit on a traditional contract. In some companies this last point is overcome by recruiting from outside for the non-traditional types of contract. It is interesting that these contracts are often run quite separately and located in a separate division from the normal contracting activities.

The third way of differentiating the product is by putting together financial packages. These ensure the go-ahead for large-scale projects which are beyond the financial capacity of a client or where the client prefers not to finance it himself. They are also used to finance large projects where the contractors are the initiators but where on their own they cannot or do not wish to carry the financial risk involved. Each of these may entail the provision of short-term finance while the project is under way or long-term equity finance. Financial packages are relevant to projects both in the UK and abroad. One or two of the companies visited also mentioned that where large projects were concerned and especially in the case of those for foreign clients, the size and reputation of their company (particularly where it was a well-diversified group with a strong financial asset base) was advantageous when bidding for or negotiating contracts of this type. A number of companies are working towards equipping themselves better to offer these financial packages by, for example, recruiting relevant experts. They regard these packages as an extension of their product range and as a very useful marketing tool in an economic climate which favours private investment in types of assets which previously would have been publicly owned.

Ramsay points out that '[the competitive advantage of the firm] is not related to the quality of the end product itself but includes aspects of the total business process where it enjoys an edge over its competitors in packaging, distribution or purchasing' (p. 12). The decision as to which of the two basic strategies of low cost or product differentiation to follow is important. Some companies try to do both and finish up with neither a cost advantage nor any distinctive wares.

Construction companies are in a large number of markets. They may be differentiating many of their products but most are also keeping a foot in the price-dominant markets. Because there are so many markets dominated by one-off projects, this may not be a disadvantage, as Ramsay would claim.

Ramsay has an interesting final comment on competition. He observes that:

> This theory to date has been dominated by economics. It has been suggested[4] that biology may be more relevant than economics in the development of a useful competitive theory. This starts from Darwin's conclusions that the struggle for survival is more severe among species with the same characteristics than with different characteristics. 'No two competitors can coexist who make their living in the same way. Their relationship is unstable. One will displace the other.'[5] Each business firm, in order to survive, must determine the boundaries of its particular position so that it does not compete on identical terms. In this respect, contracting is not an exception. Each contractor must determine the skills he has to offer, and what sustainable advantages he can create versus his competition. Theory is easy to write, much more difficult to put into practice. In strategy, there is often a wide gap between planning and implementation. The best plan is only a plan unless it degenerates into work[6] (p. 27, reference numbers altered).

2.3.4 Synergy

Synergy in business arises when 'various parts or processes of the firm can combine together to create something greater than simply the actual sum of the parts'.

Cannon and Hillebrandt in the chapter on diversification in the companion volume distinguish three types of synergy: operating, management and investment.[7] They also refer to synergy in sales. Of those, it is in operating and management that they suggest that synergy may be very strong. The interviews did not provide much evidence either of the potential for synergy or of attempts by firms to exploit that potential if it existed. There were one or two exceptions.

About a quarter of the companies interviewed are taking steps to break down the barriers between various activities usually run by separate operating units. They considered that greater links could produce benefits to the group in the products they could offer and in improving their capability. There was however no claim that the benefits would be greater than the sum of the two types of expertise.

In more than one company there had been a failure to appreciate at an early stage that the use of computers purchased for one purpose could be used to improve the efficiency of other parts of the organisation. There were one or two examples where putting together specialist expertise with computers had enabled elaborate design capability to be developed beyond expectations. In these cases synergy could be said to exist.

In all industries, however, it is possible to sustain a synergistic effect by putting together a team where the contribution to problem solving, for example, or increasing efficiency by the whole team exceeds the sum of the contributions of individual members. This is one of the reasons why a committee or task-force approach may be beneficial. This seems a particularly relevant area in construction whose crucial resource is management and which involves the ability to work effectively with other members of the construction team.

2.4   STRATEGIC PLANNING

All the companies visited undertake some form of strategic planning. Several companies have been making some strategic plans since the 1960s though some have done so only very recently. Before the 1960s there was emphasis on numerical planning but when the market environment changed dramatically this led to disillusionment and to a rejection of this approach except for the short term. After a lapse of time a more qualitative approach was adopted for the longer term of five years or more. In more than one company the introduction of strategic planning was the result of recommendations by management consultants or other advisers.

The way in which objectives and strategies are formulated varies considerably. In some cases the main boards of companies together with certain other senior management set aside two or more days to consider the way in which they wish the company to develop and to draw up and spell out objectives. The resulting document is then given to all top management personnel and the broad outline is communicated to other senior management by the chairman.

In other cases the objectives of each part of the organisation are developed separately as part of the planning process and then collated and considered at divisional level. The main board operates at a different level of company objectives and there seemed little feedback from the board to divisions or from the divisions upwards or downwards. Thus the planning document which includes objectives is not used as a blueprint for action.

In one company the chairman is the prime mover in determining the overall direction of the group and his broad objectives are linked with the bottom-up approach from the component parts of the business in the five-year plan.

One of the reasons why planning has been neglected by contractors in the past – and to some extent still is – is that the capital base of the industry is low so that it is not necessary to plan for large investments in fixed assets. Another reason is that until recently they saw themselves as having no control over their markets and as simply having to respond to client calls for tender. The first reason is largely invalidated by the fact that it is management which is their scarce resource and that it is as necessary to plan for the proper use of existing management, and for the acquisition or the internal development of new management, as it is for manufacturing industry to plan for new plant. In the 1960s companies were less aware of this fact than they are now. The second reason is invalidated not only by the fact that contractors do have a choice of markets in which to operate, but also by the recent opportunities to develop new projects by organising financial packages and by the realisation that it is possible to market the expertise of the company even though it is difficult to influence the size of the market for their type of product (see Chapter 5 for a discussion on this point). Nevertheless a number of companies were keen that the planning process should not be a strait-jacket which in any way discouraged the grasping of unexpected opportunities which presented themselves.

The time-horizon of strategic planning varies widely among the large firms visited. Longer-term strategic goals – for, say, five years or so – are sometimes formulated at main board level but sometimes originate in the divisions of the group. In one company the main board determines broad policy for the group while the subsidiary companies vary in the extent of their strategic planning, some going to about five years ahead in considerable depth. In one company 'we plan for five years and dream for the next five'.

Several companies plan for three years ahead. The scope of the business in type and geographical spread of work, possible acquisitions, the level of profits, innovation and change, market share, productivity, financial and physical resources and management performance and development are some of the subjects covered. Most plans assume a constant external environment in terms of the economy and the government. These plans originate either at the main board level or at the individual subsidiary or divisional level but the detail has to be provided by the latter.

There are defects in the three-year approach in companies where the larger projects from inception to completion span a period well in excess of three years. Any attempt to change the direction in which the company or part of the company is moving cannot necessarily be fully implemented within so short a time-scale. For instance if a company wishes to diversify into a new activity, it may have the good fortune to buy a company with the necessary expertise. If not it will take a longer time to recruit or develop and market the necessary skills (see Chapter 3, Section 3.3).

Whether it originates at board level and is then passed down for detailed infilling or whether it starts at activity level and is brought together at board level, amended and sent back to activity level later does not seem to be crucial to the success of the planning operation. What does seem to be very important is that the plans should be communicated to, and discussed with, all those charged with their implementation in detail or in broad terms. This does not always happen. Indeed in one company a person with responsibility for marketing who had been appointed for some months had not even seen the group plan. In some companies it was felt that the strategic plan was something that had to be made because it had been so decreed by the board but it was not regarded as the working document to help and guide management at all levels. 'Managers find the five-year plan irrelevant. To them it is next year which matters.' In another company the attitude was that 'if you force people to think longer-term it takes their mind off immediate problems'. In another company it was remarked that 'the use of the plan depends on the personality and attitudes of individual managers. It should give them a very clear idea of what the company intends to do.' Unless the strategic plan is communicated to all relevant persons and unless these persons accept and support it fully as a blueprint for action it is not fulfilling its whole purpose.

Because the external and internal environments change rapidly any plan which is a blueprint for action needs to be frequently updated. In most companies it was updated each year; in a few it was reviewed every six months.

In many companies planning is seen as an extension of the budgeting process which is the means of control on the financial side of the business and this may be one of the reasons for the earlier emphasis on numerical long-term planning. Budgets are prepared for a minimum of one year ahead and sometimes eighteen months or two years. They are reviewed at regular intervals – often quarterly. In a number of cases the budgets include a planning statement on market targets, special opportunities, etc., and in some cases cover the whole philosophy of the operating unit: where it is, where it wants to be and how it proposes to get there. This is a misunderstanding of the role of the budget which should be a tool for control of resources. The broader assessment constitutes planning.

The budgeting process and its distinct character in the contracting business is discussed in Chapter 4.

2.5 THE DEVELOPMENT OF STRATEGIC THINKING

Contractors now generally regard formal consideration of the strategy of their businesses as a central function within their organisation. There is however no overt attempt to put strategic decisions in a conceptual framework and it might be helpful to senior management to be exposed to academic thinking on this matter, for example, by inviting speakers to give occasional lectures. At the moment only those going on some courses would be aware of the theory. Better acquaintance with the concepts developed by Ramsay and others would be beneficial to most companies interviewed. In those companies which have well-developed strategic and planning systems it might give managers some confidence to know that they are acting according to established modern management thinking. For those companies groping to improve their strategic planning it might give valuable guidance on how to think about and implement the process.

The acceptance of the need for formulation of strategy and for planning in the second half of the 1980s is in contrast to the situation of the 1970s and even more so to that of the 1960s when very few companies were beginning to think strategically. The reason for this change stems largely from those which have been taking place in the industry and in the environment in which they operate, some of which are mentioned in Chapter 1.

First, work became more difficult to obtain in the wake of the traumatic drop in work in the UK from 1974. The fall in public sector work, which included the bulk of civil engineering work, was not halted until 1981 and its adverse impact on large construction firms was reinforced by the completion of the construction of concrete oil platforms destined for North Sea exploration and the drop in work abroad, especially in the Middle East. As a result of these events profit margins fell and contractors were forced to control their

operations more carefully. Strategic planning was one of the frame-
works in which they considered the options open to them and how
they could best act to cope with the leaner times in which they found
themselves.

At the same time technologies were changing – for example,
engineering services were becoming more important; steel frames
could now be used more readily in buildings and new cladding
materials and methods were developed. All this led to a possibility of
faster building and to a need for more specialists on site.[8] This
coincided with increasing pressures from developers for a reduction
in the duration of construction because of the heavy financial costs
involved with the larger scale of many developments.

Greater complexity and speed combined with an increase in size of
the largest schemes imposed a greater load on management and this
is one of the reasons for the change in the arrangements for the
construction process – the increase in subcontracting, the development of management contracting and other non-traditional ways of
organising construction. Contractors were forced to consider which
of these new services they would offer and this became a component
of their planning operations.

At the same time the structure of the industry was changing in that
some companies had been taken over by conglomerates. These were
used to planning in their other businesses and insisted on a plan as
part of their control mechanism. They set financial targets which
needed careful planning for their achievement.

As Ramsay observes 'In this process [of concentration and diver-
sification] companies are effectively changing the scope of their
business by redefining their competitive position within the industry,
and are looking for effective segments or niches within the total
market' (p. 24).

Once a majority of companies were undertaking some sort of
planning the others tended to follow suit. They were often prodded
into it by outside advisers, sometimes forced into it by losses in parts
of their business, and helped all the time by an increased awareness
of various management techniques including planning. The last was
sometimes introduced into the company either by newly recruited
senior staff or by executive or non-executive directors who had
experience of planning elsewhere.

It is a result of all these pressures that strategic planning has come
to play a major part in policy-making by large construction firms
although in a number of companies it has yet to be fully developed.

Ramsay in his chapter said that 'It needs to be stressed however that the companies generally regarded as the most successful in terms of sales, growth, profitability and returns have well-defined strategies'[9] (p. 13, reference number altered).

The interviews were not sufficiently deep to be able to make this positive statement about the companies concerned. What can be said however is that those companies which had unsatisfactory performance were those which had poor strategy and planning.

(The most relevant chapter in the companion volume is chapter 2; see Appendix to this volume.)

NOTES AND REFERENCES

1. Ramsay, W., 'Business Objectives and Strategy' in Hillebrandt, P.M. and Cannon, J. (eds) *The Management of Construction Firms: Aspects of Theory* (London: Macmillan, 1989) ch. 2. This source is repeatedly quoted in this chapter and is indicated by page or section numbers.
2. Ansoff, H.I., *Corporate Strategy: An Analytical Approach to Business Policy for Growth and Expansion* (New York: McGraw Hill, 1965).
3. Barry, H. 'Strategy and the Business Portfolio' *Long Range Planning*, vol. 10, no 1 (February 1977) pp. 9–15 for more detail on the growth-share matrix.
4. Henderson, B. *The Logic of Business Strategy* (Cambridge, Mass: Ballinger, 1984) pp. 15–25.
5. Ibid, p. 20, note 3. This is Gause's law of mutual exclusion.
6. Drucker, P.F., *Management: Tasks, Responsibilities, Practices* (New York: Harper & Row, 1973).
7. Cannon, J. and Hillebrandt, P.M., 'Diversification' in Hillebrandt, P.M. and Cannon, J. (eds) *The Management of Construction Firms: Aspects of Theory* (London: Macmillan, 1989) ch. 3, p. 39.
8. National Economic Development Office (NEDO) *Faster Building for Commerce* (London: NEDO, 1988) para 3.2.
9. Harvey, D.F., *Cases in Business Policy and Strategic Management* (Merrill, 1983). Pp. 21, 22 list eight different studies which support the favourable results of strategic planning.

3 Growth and Diversification

3.1 INTRODUCTION

The chapter on diversification in the companion volume established the theoretical framework to diversification decisions and underlined the major reasons for the different approaches of construction companies to diversification, when compared with those met in other industries.

Diversification is defined as the process by which firms extend the range of their business operations outside those in which they are currently engaged. This broad definition includes (a) the process referred to as backward vertical integration, that is, the acquisition or development of businesses whose products are inputs to the firm's own main operations; (b) forward integration, that is, the extension of the firm's activities to those of the normal purchase of its products; (c) horizontal diversification, that is, a movement into other markets not involving the firm in any vertical relationships as in (a) and (b) above. Any of these forms of expansion may take place either by internal development or by merger or takeover[1] (p. 31).

In this chapter the focus is first on growth policy, which is often the main trigger for diversification. The main part of the chapter thus deals with reasons for diversification by construction companies as well as by corporations into construction businesses. Finally, some of the reasons why diversification may not take place are considered.

3.2 GROWTH

The advantages of large size were implicitly appreciated in many discussions and in at least one case spelt out quite precisely:

Size is important for three reasons – first, because the size of project is large and often needs to be financed as well as actually undertaken on the building site; secondly because size gives confidence to the client in the capability of the company, and thirdly because the increase in facilities enables a spread of risk and also enables good ideas to be put into practice.

Underlying this statement is the belief that large size in construction facilitates growth, and growth in some form or other is the openly avowed purpose of all those who took part in the interviews. In a number of cases, growth is interpreted as that of the particular activities for which individuals were responsible rather than growth for the group as a whole. Indeed, it is only at board level that discussions on growth targets, the means to achieve them and the difficulties likely to be met are tackled in both a general and detailed manner. It is also at board level that the major reasons for diversifying outside contracting are iterated. In the contracting divisions of the companies visited the emphasis is squarely on how to achieve targets agreed with the board. There is no concern for growth likely to be achieved by the company as a whole where it is well diversified except in the sense of irritation at the fact that in the 1980s it had seemed easier to achieve high profits and growth rates in housebuilding and commercial development than in contracting.

3.2.1 Measurement and objectives of growth

The process of growth of a firm can be measured in a number of ways. The valuation of assets in the balance sheet is one. Another is obtained by examining the turnover of the firm. Yet another is the trend in profits. The change in the number of employees may also be used as a proxy measure, though it is of limited worth (see Chapter 8). First, a firm may become larger by increasing its asset base, which in turn may require fewer employees. Second, if a firm shifts increasingly towards the use of self-employed labour the concomitant will be a smaller workforce, though not a smaller firm.

Yet another way to assess growth is to monitor changes in Stock Exchange share prices. However, the latter may move up or down for reasons which have nothing whatever to do with the perception of the instrinsic true worth of the company.

Another difficulty relates to the treatment of inflation. Since, in many company accounts, no allowance is made for the effect of inflation, growth cannot be measured accurately for different types of activity, and hence for the company as a whole. Even turnover presents difficulties in interpretation, as it does not have the same meaning as in other industries where turnover and sales can be equated. In contracting, turnover is made up of part-payments for work which is measured at regular intervals and of final payments, some of which may be higher or lower than the provisional assessment. The use of subcontractors also makes turnover a suspect index of size and growth. There is therefore a degree of uncertainty attached to turnover which does not exist in companies where the final price of the products is not in doubt and where turnover represents the sale of completed goods.

Growth objectives, because they are discussed mainly at board level, thus tend to be described in terms of their overall rate, rather than those for individual parts of the company. They are stated in commercial terms based on profits and not turnover. Because of the low asset base of contracting, even when a construction company is well diversified into capital-intensive businesses, growth objectives tend to be expressed in terms of rising profits rather than in terms of a larger asset valuation. Companies monitor the achievements of competitors though it is not always possible for them to compare their relative successes in different parts of their businesses because companies are not required to report their annual statements and accounts in a way which identifies the scale and results of individual types of activities.

3.2.2 Means of growth

Since the accent is very much on increased profits rather than increased turnover *per se*, it was emphasised in a number of companies that an increase in profits did not necessarily require a rise in turnover, but could be achieved by greater efficiency and tighter control on costs. It should be obvious, however, that these economies are available in the short term only.

Where the potential for higher profits simply through more efficient use of resources seems poor, the alternatives are internal or external growth, that is, increases in the volume of contracting work or in the level of activity of existing businesses, whether or not related to contracting in the construction chain, or through the acquisition of or merger with other companies, whether or not related to existing activities. All those who were interviewed accepted that both methods had to be pursued although it seemed that in some cases, internal growth was sought in a more planned and organised manner than was external growth where a number of companies were content to wait until suitable opportunities became known to them rather than seek them out aggressively.

3.2.3 Reasons for growth

The advantages of growth in the contracting part of the company are seen by board members mainly in terms of the increased cash flow which would thus be available to fund additional investments in its capital-hungry businesses or in those of the corporation of which it is part. An additional benefit from growth was seen in the opportunities for promotion which it offered. 'If you don't expand, you bottle up opportunities for young people. If you don't attract young people, you choke the company.'

Other reasons for external growth of the contracting side of the business include the desire to become a multinational type of business in the sense of operations in a larger number of regions in the world. This is a type of horizontal diversification. The move into other geographical areas might also be spurred by poor prospects for growth in those areas where the company was established or by the need for wider types of markets. One firm said that it was unlikely to be able to maintain its historical growth because of the limitations of the market-place in which it was operating. Organic growth was considered to be too slow for the rapidly changing industry and this is one reason for mergers and takeovers.

Mention was also made of the fact that, where some companies faced difficulties and sought a buyer, it gave the purchaser an opportunity to expand his crucial management resource. Another reason given was that purchase of, or merger with, another company can be the quicker and more efficient way of acquiring skills and expertise, either absent or in short supply in-house, or to develop a better balance of related activities and thus offer a better service to clients. Managerial slack – that is, spare management resources within some functions – could also be a motivating factor in growth policy.

Senior managers should be able to assess the reasons why diversification into certain types of industries is more appropriate than into others, so far as the construction industry is concerned, and why a contracting business is attractive as a component of a conglomerate. They should be aware of and appreciate the advantages and the problems associated with growth and diversification and understand the differences between contracting and manufacturing industry in these respects. These matters were certainly not sufficiently understood by some senior managers in the firms surveyed nor were they necessarily stimulated to enquire for themselves.

In no firm had there been an attempt to broaden the knowledge of the professionals which make up the cohort of top managers to include those aspects of economics and financial theory relevant to the construction industry. In at least one case diversification moves by the main board were seen as a direct threat to the long-term prospects of a senior manager on the contracting side. This is an example of communication mechanisms being patently inadequate and in this instance it was compounded by a lack of understanding of the reasons for a diversification strategy.

Both types of failures can be easily remedied: the former by ensuring that not only are major investments or other changes announced in good time, but also that the reasons for doing so are fully explained; the latter can be remedied by attendance at a relevant in-house or external short course.

3.3 MEANS OF GROWTH AND DIVERSIFICATION

Since diversification (the move by a company into a type of activity not undertaken by it) is one way to achieve growth, the means to implement growth and diversification policies are considered here together. Not surprisingly, for public limited companies, there is a concern with the views and the valuations by Stock Exchange analysts. This is further developed in Chapter 4.

Essentially there are two routes which are open to companies seeking to develop their own businesses or to move into new ones. These are by internal or external means. Internal means refer to the development of additional in-house capacity where growth of existing activities is concerned, or of new skills, expertise and production facilities in the case of diversification. External means refer to the acquisition of existing businesses. Chapter 3 in the companion book deals with these in detail.

In external diversification, depending on the financial circumstances of the company undertaking the purchase, settlement may be made by cash, by the issue of shares or by a combination of both. In construction companies with a large cash positive contracting side, purchase for cash may be the preferred choice. This will certainly be the case for family-controlled firms which do not wish to see their shareholdings in the business diluted in any way. Conversely, in corporations, diversification will on the whole be financed by a share issue.

Both internal and external means to growth and diversification have different implications for the companies in terms of the integration and development of the relevant activities.

The development of new activities by in-house means, which involves recruitment of specialist manpower and management, purchase and installation of equipment and other inputs to the new process, will in all cases be slower than the purchase of a business. There is also risk of failure, because barriers to entry may not have been correctly assessed, thus leading to greater costs or difficulties than anticipated.

The advantage of buying a company as opposed to developing the group's own expertise is largely a matter of time. It is a long process to become a known and respected business in a particular geographical area or type of work. On the other hand buying a company does involve risk and therefore policy is to take a long look at a company before purchase. The group has had no major surprises though, on occasions, the strengths of a company were not exactly as envisaged.

On the other hand, the purchase of a business also has some inherent disadvantages. However detailed and penetrating the analysis of the business to be bought by the purchasing company, it may fail to discover some feature in the former which will make commercial success of the new venture less likely. Where, as is so often the case, management is the crucial resource in the proposed acquisition, difficulties arise if those with specialist know-how subsequently leave the new company. At least one large construction company mentioned this as a reason for extra care when considering acquisitions as well as a reason for allowing those acquisitions to lead a largely independent existence. Several companies commented on their policies in this respect, for example:

In general for contracting there are substantial problems in acquisition, first of assessment and secondly of assimilation. The assets of a contractor are his management and his workload; in acquiring a contractor there is a danger that the management may turn out not to be as good as expected or managers may leave the company once it has been acquired. The workload is difficult to assess. Indeed it is difficult to assess the value of the workload of a company which you own, let alone the workload of a company which you are hoping to acquire. There is in any case the disruption and problems of morale which arise and the difficulty of assimilating the new organisation within the culture of the old.

It is policy, after acquisition of a company, to let it run itself for a while. This has a number of advantages: first it retains managers, secondly, if the performance is not good there is no question of blaming the takeover and thirdly it enables the group managers to assess the situation and problems over time.

3.4 EXTENT OF DIVERSIFICATION

All the large contracting companies have diversified out of contracting into other types of construction activity, notably property development and housing. Many of them have decided to diversify out of construction into other activities, some still related to construction in some way but others in quite separate industries. Table 1.3 in Chapter 1 gives some indication of the span of activities but does not reflect the great diversity of the activities which include, for example, manufacture of boats, computer software and gold-mining. Nor does it show that while contracting remains the core of the business so far as turnover (though not necessarily profit) is concerned, diversification into non-construction activities has gone far in a few of the companies. This is understandable because few annual accounts split turnover into that from each category of business. In a few of the cases shown in Table 1.2 the construction turnover includes a substantial proportion of activities which have virtually no connection with construction, just because no breakdown of turnover is available. Thus the apparent proportion of construction activities is overstated.

Of all the companies interviewed only one could really be described as concentrating its activities on contracting though this company also had important property and housing interests, and its concentration on the core business of construction was a deliberate decision. Most companies have kept the largest part of their activities in the construction business in its broad interpretation which includes, in addition to housing and property, materials production, manufacture of temporary buildings, plant, merchandising and so on. A few have deliberately decided to have only a relatively small proportion of their business in construction-related activities and to diversify out of construction for the remainder of their work. However, the choice of areas for diversification is difficult. One company said 'Our policy is evolutionary. It always starts from something we know how to do well.' Another said:

> It is group policy that most diversification should be in areas away from construction, but where the group has some knowledge. It is difficult to find such businesses which fulfil the other criteria of avoidance of construction cycles and high-technology-type markets. To a small extent however this has been achieved, not so much as a result of deliberate policy, but because the group owned a few businesses where development has been possible.

3.5 REASONS FOR DIVERSIFICATION

Reasons for diversification by contractors into construction or non-construction activities may be considered in five groups. The first, discussed in Section 3.2 above, is the aim to increase profitable growth and to seek different activities in which this may be achieved. The second group of reasons includes those to increase efficiency as discussed in Section 3.5.1 below. The third is financial – see Section 3.5.2. The fourth group is connected with improving the security of the firm – see Section 3.5.3. Lastly there is the diversification which takes place for some extraneous reason. This may be the purchase of a company in the construction business which has some other non-contracting business as a subsidiary, the personal interest of a senior executive of the company or an attractive offer of a business through personal connections.

Each of these aims may find a solution in vertical or horizontal diversification. In the companion volume two reasons were selected as most important for vertical integration in construction: (i) market failure – that is, that market forces do not provide the requirements of the industry at the right place, time, price, quality and quantity; and (ii) uncertainty.

Two reasons for horizontal diversification were also selected as of special significance. First, there is the secular decline in parts of the market. Second, there is:

a need for contracting companies to spread risks and especially to reduce fluctuations in their output which may be either seasonal or cyclical. Ideally, diversification ought to be into products or geographical markets with a pattern of demand counter-cyclical to that in which contracting companies are already operating. This is difficult to achieve, and an alternative is to diversify into a market where demand is relatively stable (companion volume, p. 39).

3.5.1 Increased efficiency

One method of achieving increased efficiency is by controlling the source of supply of materials to avoid erratic or long delivery times, high prices or poor quality, or in other words to avoid market failure. When a group purchases a material company it is diversifying vertically and backwards. In this case the contractor himself becomes the customer of the new venture for at least part of its output and understands what the product should be. There are many examples of this process. One is a contractor who was in the business of testing equipment to the specifications required. He bought an instrument-making company to ensure the supply. A very common example is where a contractor goes into the business of producing aggregates because he has a large road construction project. In this case it may be very short-term diversification because he may divest himself of the aggregate business at the end of the road contract or he may retain it and extend it.

Another form of backward vertical integration is the acquisition of subcontractors who would normally be supplying a service to the main contractor. Generally contractors were not very enthusiastic about this idea though, in earlier periods, a number of specialist firms, for example, heating and ventilating engineers, had been acquired. Since the trend in the industry generally at the moment is towards a greater amount of subcontracting rather than having the skills in-house the time may not be appropriate for this type of diversification.

It is a different matter, however, when it is felt desirable to add to the existing activities of a company one which is complementary, such as the linking of a mechanical services specialist to an electrical services specialist or one strong in the north of the country with one strong in the south. This is horizontal diversification.

3.5.2 Financial efficiency

One of the characteristics of contracting is that it generates a positive cash flow. One company mentioned that a third of its profits came from interest on cash available during the contract period and other companies indicated that interest earned was an important source of profit (see also Chapter 4). Provided that the positive cash flow of contracting activities continues at a fairly even rate there is no reason why the cash should not be invested in other operations of the company instead of being lodged with financial institutions and these can represent either vertical or horizontal diversification. Thus contractors have invested in cash-hungry businesses both in the general construction field and outside it. The principal directions of diversification within the broad construction orbit are speculative housebuilding and property development where in both cases considerable funds are required for land holding and in financing the building during the construction phase and until it is sold. In some cases contractors have retained their investment in properties, to strengthen their asset base or as an additional source of diversification and investment. Cash may also be used in any business which is more capital-intensive than construction and this applies, for example, to material production, such as aggregates, and to almost any manufacturing industry.

Movement by a contractor into any business with a more substantial holding of fixed assets is beneficial in terms of stock exchange valuations. The only really valuable assets a contractor has are his goodwill, his management team and his work in progress. The first two are difficult to value and can, as already mentioned, disperse very rapidly if the company has problems, the last may be valuable but is uncertain until the contracts are completed. Stockbrokers, therefore, tend to be favourably impressed by an increase in the book value of assets in the balance sheet of a company which can be achieved by holdings of land, factories, etc.

However, not all changes are made in this direction. One company decided that because its contracting operations were undervalued by the stock market, the group as a whole was badly undervalued in spite of profitable and valuable property holdings. It decided to split the construction company from the property company and since then the rating of both has improved. The original situation was a sort of negative synergy – that is, the sum of the parts together was less than the total of the individual parts.

3.5.3 Greater security

One of the major disadvantages of contracting is that because the large firms in the industry construct buildings and other works which are investment goods the demand for their output is subject to wide fluctuations of a cyclical nature. To this have been added fluctuations in UK public-sector demand resulting from attempts by government in the 1960s and 1970s to 'manage' the economy and from the government policy of steadily reducing public sector involvement in the mid-1970s. There are difficulties in finding an industry which does not follow a cyclical trend at least to some extent and indeed many industries suffer fluctuations in demand as great as those in construction. One way in which contractors have created a more stable situation is by securing the demand for a new product over several years by long-term contracts to purchase. Notable is coal production where contracts in the UK with the Coal Board and the electricity industry to produce certain quantities at an agreed price over a period of years give stability to the contractor's market. This has been repeated with major customers in other mineral-mining operations to overcome the problems of fluctuations on the world markets for these products. Another way of overcoming the problem of economic cycles is to spread operations round the world so that at least the ups and downs of national cycles do not necessarily coincide. Thus contractors have gone into housebuilding in the USA, Canada and Spain where the housebuilding cycles in those countries do not necessarily follow those of the UK. Some activities selected by contractors have lesser cycles than construction, for example, instrument production. Others, such as DIY outlets, though construction-related, do not necessarily follow the cycles of large construction projects.

Apart from the risks inherent in cyclical demand patterns there is always a risk in being closely connected to one industry and diversification has been regarded as a means of spreading risks for these general reasons too. To overcome both this problem and that of cyclical fluctuations diversification is likely to be horizontal rather than vertical because vertical diversification, almost by definition, is likely to have the same cycles as the original business.

Another reason for diversification mentioned by at least one firm was the risk attached to too high a degree of dependence on the demands by a particular type of client, in this case the public sector. It was strongly felt that risk in this case was no longer associated with the inevitability of cycles, but rather with lack of long-term growth prospects.

3.6 DIVERSIFICATION INTO CONSTRUCTION

Diversification is not merely a one-way option for construction companies. Over the years, a number of large corporations have taken over construction companies to complement some of their other activities or to strengthen the financial base of those corporations whose businesses are largely concentrated in technologically advanced industries, which are cash-hungry. Contracting, which if well managed, should produce a positive cash flow, is a particularly attractive type of activity to a company which seeks to deepen its asset base.

There are other aspects of a construction company which may attract a large corporation. They include a diversified portfolio of properties and a good land bank. Both will obviously strengthen the corporate balance sheet, the former enabling the property portfolio to be used to raise loans to further the company's growth plans and the latter in particular to provide the opportunity for further profitable developments. Both the size of the corporation and its ranking in the corporate league may enable it to raise the funds for development more cheaply and more easily than the construction company on its own. To that extent, diversification into construction benefits both parties in the process.

3.7 BARRIERS TO DIVERSIFICATION

Most companies wish to grow but not all wish to diversify. Indeed there may be good reasons not to do so. However, even a vague wish to diversify is not sufficient for it requires an adventurous main board with a wish to expand and a willingness to take risks before a policy of diversification can be successfully implemented. The lack of this combination of attributes in a firm is the ultimate barrier to diversification.

There is a considerable risk in moving from construction into a completely new market. The know-how required to manage a contracting business is different from that in manufacturing and it may well be that the type of manager who has grown up in the contracting business will have considerable difficulty in managing in a manufacturing or extraction industry with, for example, its greater fixed assets and the pace of operations dictated by machines rather than men. Yet many contractors have taken this step and while the management of the original company may be retained yet the mainly contracting-oriented members of the main board must learn about the different businesses. Though it may now appear that the businesses into which contractors have diversified are completely different and separate, in many instances the progress into other industries has been by several stages, each stage having some connection with the previous one. Deep mining for minerals is an example. Several companies are in the business of open-cast coal production – some of them since the immediate post-war period. The original reason for this was the common plant in use in civil engineering and in open-cast coal production especially at the stage of removing the overburden before coal production could commence. The civil engineering contractors often owned the plant and had the operatives and know-how to manage what is basically a major muck-shifting operation. Now the process and the plant used are different. However, having got into the open-cast coal industry, connections were developed with the industry at large and with its customers and it did not seem too large a step to move into deep coal-mining. Once the know-how of deep mining had been acquired, it again did not seem too large a step to move into the deep mining of other minerals. This is an example of the way that some companies have moved into completely separate industries from contracting, with no common resources or clients, by steps which at the time were in some way connected.

Given the wish and competence to diversify there are often severe financial barriers to its implementation. While contracting generates a positive cash flow the acquisition of companies may well require greater resources than the available cash. In a public company it will be possible to raise more capital only if the share is well valued. Similarly an exchange of shares will not be acceptable to the vendor of a company unless the shares are well regarded.

The family-controlled firm has a further problem in that if it issues more shares the percentage of the total equity held by the family will fall and ultimately with this process the family may well lose control. Thus, in the case of a family business, diversification – and indeed growth – has to be internal or by small purchases financed from the available cash within the company. This places a severe limit on the extent to which these firms can expand and still remain as family businesses.

The construction firm within a conglomerate is often precluded by the parent company from going into other business especially those in which the parent company already has an operating subsidiary. Thus some contracting companies owned by a conglomerate are prevented from diversifying into property or housebuilding because another part of the group is in this business. The limitation may even apply to movement within the contracting business from say building to civil engineering or vice versa if the conglomerate has more than one contracting subsidiary.

(The most relevant chapter in the companion volume is Chapter 3; see Appendix in this volume).

NOTE AND REFERENCE

1. Cannon, J. and Hillebrandt, P.M., 'Diversification' in Hillebrandt, P.M. and Cannon, J. (eds) *The Management of Construction Firms: Aspects of Theory* (London: Macmillan, 1989) ch. 3. This source is often quoted and is indicated by page or section numbers.

4 Financial Policy

4.1 INTRODUCTION

In order to explain the various elements which make up the financial policies of the firms which were visited, it is important to differentiate between three groups:

1. the companies which are contracting businesses and part of large corporations;
2. those which are mainly involved in contracting but are public limited companies in their own right;
3. those which in one way or another – that is, in terms of ownership or management – can still be described as 'family firms'.

Financial policy in large construction firms is particularly interesting inasmuch as one of its main aims, unlike that of capital-intensive and hence cash-hungry firms, is to find suitable outlets for a positive cash flow which is not required within the contracting side of the business. At the same time all large construction firms now have a diversified structure so that those visited undertook a range of activities, which may require the raising of capital in one form or another in the future. The diversified nature of the top companies with major construction interests is illustrated in Chapter 1, Table 1.3. The more diversified a company, the more it is likely to have raised capital for long-term investment by the issue of shares or to have to do so in the future. This is not to denigrate the usefulness of a positive cash flow from the contracting side of a company but to emphasise that beyond a certain level of development, a positive cash flow on its own is insufficient to sustain the rate of expansion of some companies. It should also be pointed out that the disadvantage of a low level of fixed assets is that because the asset base is low it is difficult to raise funds on the stock market and the company has no assets on which to fall back in case of losses or low profits.

4.2 REQUIREMENTS FOR AND SOURCES OF FUNDS

As Chapter 5 of the companion volume indicates, firms typically have two quite different requirements for funds. The first is short-term, and is typically met by bank overdrafts. The second is long-term, and its purpose is to help finance the growth objectives of the firm (see Chapter 3). The sources of funds can also be internal, where retained profits and depreciation make up the total available for investment.

4.2.1 Short-term finance

Overdraft facilities are arranged with banks in order to deal with fluctuations in the level of funds required to meet expenditure on labour and management, materials and components and other recurring types of expenditure. Large firms, which undertake most of the large projects, may well be faced nowadays with a rising requirement for working capital in order to ensure that the stock of materials to be used for the project is adequate to enable construction to proceed at the required pace. The more sophisticated and technologically advanced a building or structure, the larger the level of expenditure which is needed to finance the purchase of the inputs and, *ceteris paribus*, the larger the level of overdraft facilities which a firm will wish to arrange in order to cope with the inevitable short-term fluctuations in the company's cash flow. Moreover, it has become more difficult to maintain the volume of cash flow to earlier levels. One contractor speaking of a rather specialised business said

The business used to be self-funding but this has changed because of four factors:

1. lower profit margins which are in some cases slim or non-existent;
2. inflation is lower and this, following a period of high inflation which allows laxity in financial practices, means that tightening up is necessary;
3. more fixed price contracts;
4. more difficult credit terms.

4.2.2 Long-term finance

One of the sources of long-term finance in construction companies is a positive cash flow from contracting operations. This arises because a contractor is able to obtain payments for past work even though he may not yet have had to pay for materials and subcontracted labour. It is this particular feature of the contracting side of the industry which differentiates it from manufacturing industry. Even in management contracting the cash flow is positive and the fee accrues evenly, is reliable and has a low risk.

Since contracting is essentially labour-intensive, there is little call for funds to finance investment in capital – that is, plant and equipment, either new or replacement.

Depreciation is therefore also a relatively minor item in the contracting firm's profit and loss account. Efficiency in terms of making the best use of the financial resources available to the firm thus calls for diverting them away from where there is a surplus of funds to where they can earn a higher return than the ruling interest rate. The only justification for keeping liquid funds is in the expectation that an opportunity for investing them will arise shortly or when the interest earned is higher than could be earned if invested elsewhere. This was indeed the case in at least one company.

One firm claimed that one of the advantages of large size was that large projects generated a greater contribution to the company's cash flow than did a number of smaller contracts totalling the same value. In another firm, it was claimed that a substantial share of the net profits arising from individual well-managed projects could be attributed to the interest earned on the positive cash flow which they generated.

In general, the fact that most operating divisions or subsidiary companies are credited with the interest earned by the company on the cash flow which they generate tends to demonstrate the importance attached to them by the holding company on the one hand and on the other the need for operating divisions to concentrate their efforts on reinvesting it.

The positive cash flow from contracting means that diversification processes tend to focus on capital-intensive activities such as housing, where the cost of holding land banks may be heavy; development, building material production, and mining, where the purchase price of the land and that of the equipment exert heavy pressures on the financial management of the firm. The requirements for finance for these and other businesses were analysed and discussed in the companion volume and are summarised in Table 4.1. The assessments in this table were largely supported by the discussions with contractors.

These types of activities, housebuilding, development, material production and mining are particularly attractive diversification alternatives to contracting as they are cash-hungry businesses and because they enable contracting businesses to develop an asset base not available in contracting. Thus, a construction company which special-

Table 4.1 Finance required by various types of business

Purpose of finance	Type of business						
	Contracting	House building	Plant hire	Materials production	Mining	Property development	Property investment
Working capital	1	2	2	2	2	2	2
Speculative and WIP	–	3	–	2	1	3	3
Stocks ordered and WIP	1	1	1	1	1	1	–
Unexpected liabilities	3	1	2	1	3	1	2
Operating assets other than land	–	1	3	3	3	–	3
New ventures	–	1	–	2	1	2	2
Land	–	3	–	–	2	3	–

Notes: WIP = work in progress

The numbers from 1 to 3 indicate the relative importance of requirements of finance for each type of business: 1 = low; 2 = medium; 3 = high.

Source: Based on contribution by J. Stevenson in Cannon, J. and Hillebrandt, P.M., 'Financial Strategy' in Hillebrandt, P.M. and Cannon J. (eds) *Management of Large Construction Firms: Aspects of Theory* (London: Macmillan, 1989) Table 5.1.

ises in contracting will find it profitable to diversify into capital-intensive operations. It also follows that corporate firms largely engaged in capital-intensive production will seek to bring into the fold a cash-positive firm.

The family firms are in a different situation because, even though they have the same opportunities as the other two types of construction firms to generate a positive cash flow, they may be unable to raise the necessary loans for more capital-intensive activities. If they have failed to diversify they cannot offer the banks sufficiently attractive guarantees based on substantial asset value. For some firms over which 'the family' exercises financial control, diversification may be a forbidden fruit as it might entail an unacceptable dilution of the family's shareholdings and a weaker degree of control over the fortunes of the firm. Purchase of a business can be made by using internal funds, loans or by the issues of shares. The last method will reduce the shareholding of the controlling family as a percentage of the total. There is thus a strict limit on the extent to which family firms can issue shares when acquiring businesses and they will wish to maintain their shareholdings well above the danger line. For a family-type firm, growth potential may therefore be limited to that which can be financed by retained profits and loans. A family firm may have the advantage in long-term investment because there is no need to go for quick profits to control the price of shares.

Another aspect of financial strategy which may adversely affect the rate of growth of the family-type firm is where it has held on too long to the Victorian view that savings are 'good' and borrowings 'bad'. One family firm summarised the reasons for increased concern with cash and cash flow as follows:

1. the group has diversified into cash-hungry businesses;
2. it has bought up companies to increase its geographical spread;
3. inflation means there is no point in keeping cash though it earns high interest if you have it;
4. there has been a change from the Victorian attitude of not owing anything.

4.3   THE DEBT/EQUITY RATIO

The firm has a choice of financing its new developments either by loans or by issuing equity, though the latter is subject to the limi-

Table 4.2 Relation of various financial factors to debt/equity ratio

Factor	Relation to debt/equity ratio
Rate of growth of earnings	Negative
Retention percentage	Negative
Concentration of ownership and control	Positive
Size of firms	Positive (but may not take advantage of it)
Growth in assets	Positive
Business risk and earnings variability	Negative
Capital intensity	Positive
Cost of debt	Negative
Share prices	Negative
Corporate tax rate	Positive
Inflation expectations	Positive
Shortage of loanable funds	Negative

Note: Negative = factors move in opposite directions, e.g. a high rate of growth of earnings leads to a lower debt/equity ratio.
Positive = factors moving in the same direction.

Source: Cannon, J. and Hillebrandt, P.M., 'Financial Strategy' in Hillebrandt, P.M. and Cannon, J., *The Management of Contracting Firms: Aspects of Theory* (London: Macmillan, 1989) Table 5.2.

tations for family firms referred to above. In the companion volume the factors affecting the choice were discussed and analysed. It was stated that:

There are limits to the amount of debt which a firm can safely contract. Any debt involves an undertaking to pay interest. If this cost is lower than the earnings from the use of the capital then the shareholders benefit. If on the other hand it is greater, for any reason, than the earnings from the capital, then there is a drain on profits which is obviously detrimental to shareholders. The greater the risk of earnings falling, the greater is the danger to the firm of a high debt/equity ratio (p. 64).

The whole argument was summarised in a table reproduced here as Table 4.2.

The overall attitude of a number of companies (about half) to debt/equity ratio may be summarised by one contractor's remark that:

The gearing is regarded as acceptable if net borrowing is below 40 per cent of shareholders funds, at 40–50 per cent there is concern and should it go over 50 per cent, considerable worry.

Other companies in the group where some gearing is regarded as acceptable or even desirable, put slightly different figures on the categories but the sentiment was the same. There was one company that at the time of the interviews had a very high gearing ratio because of a recent merger. One of its major objectives was to bring the gearing down to 'no more than 50 per cent of shareholders' funds'.

Many of the family firms were still averse to borrowings. One which had to borrow from the banks had as one of its objectives to get this debt down to nil. Another family firm had a slightly more flexible approach but was still averse to large borrowings:

> The family is not happy with a large borrowing. At the moment, the amount of borrowing is virtually nil, but it is possible that a 20 per cent debt-to-equity ratio would be a possibility and this would be a means of acquiring some outside companies or activities if appropriate.

It is interesting that the theory as outlined in the companion volume suggests that with a concentration of ownership and control, managers would be wary of issuing new shares since it would change voting control by existing shareholders and thus weaken their job security. This does not take account of the situation in the construction industry. Where the firm is a wholly-owned subsidiary the question does not arise. In the other cases, which are all family-controlled, these are not only owned but also managed by the family. The family may in some cases be opposed to borrowing on the grounds that it increases risk too much. The theory argues that lenders are more willing to provide funds where earnings are stable and they may not be so in construction. But above all most of the theoretical arguments in the companion volume are couched in terms of managers' decisions on the assumption that managers are separate from owners. When they are not and when the owner/managers are in practice a few individuals with some non-manager family-owners' pressure behind them, the situation is quite different and the whole ethos is one of caution, with many of the other arguments on, for example, share price, cost of debt, tax rates being largely irrelevant or at least insignificant.

However, it is not only family firms which are unwilling to have a high debt/equity ratio. There are other firms, managed by persons with a very low shareholding and which have no shareholder with more than 5 per cent of the total, which also like to keep their borrowings low or nil. Indeed at the time of the interviews one or two had high cash holdings though a takeover in one case subsequently reduced these to small levels. Their reasons are much more those of the theory (see Table 4.2) but with business risk and earnings variability weighted highly as a reason for a cautious financing policy.

4.4 FINANCIAL OBJECTIVES AND MONITORING OF PERFORMANCE

The overriding financial objective met in firms is unequivocally that of 'increasing pre-tax profits'. This statement is usually complemented by an expression such as 'consistently into the future', or some such vague horizon.

It will be obvious that of the range of financial ratios discussed in Chapter 5 of the companion volume, the ratio of profit to capital employed will be largely meaningless in an organisation where the level of capital, relative to that met in manufacturing industry, is so very much lower. Indeed, in most construction firms, where contracting represents a large share of total activity, other ratios are more suitable as indices of performance. They include the ratio of profits to sales and turnover and of profits to added value.

Typically, in all companies visited, which were all diversified to a greater or lesser extent, different ratios were used to monitor the performance of the contracting side and development or manufacturing parts of the business.

All firms visited mentioned a wide-ranging set of financial data, examined in detail at board meetings, where deviation from the expected expenditure and income patterns by identifiable parts of the groups set in motion a series of actions aimed at correcting the problems.

The impression gained, however, was that although some companies rely on a well-organised and relevant set of financial data to improve financial policy, a number of them have not yet established a fully relevant set of financial criteria and systems.

They all put much emphasis on the importance of cash-generation. 'We watch slow payments'; 'We're trying to improve cash forecasting'; 'We monitor cash on a daily basis.' Some firms clearly have close and effective control. Yet it was not obvious that the correct monitoring mechanisms were operating in the various divisions of some of these large firms to ensure tight control over working capital and maximum effort towards optimal cash generation. Indeed, to several companies, cash management was a relatively recent addition to the strategy. On the whole proper attention to cash-generation seemed to be a more recent feature of financial policy in 'family' firms than in other types of firms:

> Cash-flow forecasting is not easy and not done very well because people are optimistic both as regards cash flow and performance. They cover up losses in the belief that things will get better and then they cannot cover up any longer. Over time you get to know those managers who are more reliable than others.

Another weakness which was openly discussed in a few companies was lack of standardisation in the presentation of the results of different centres of activity which made both interpretation and assessment by the board somewhat difficult.

In a number of cases an adequate flow of financial data to the board had been hampered by the delayed adoption of computerisation. It was recognised that, on the whole, the industry had been slow in waking up to the benefits from computers and that their adoption had generally been *ad hoc* and piecemeal. As a result, in a number of cases, existing systems were being evaluated with a view to determining how far they met the essential performance criteria required by companies and the extent of any necessary additional investment.

4.5   DIVIDEND POLICY

The major decision on dividend policy is how much profit to retain in the business and how much to distribute to shareholders. This is discussed under the heading of dividend policy because, once dividends are determined, the amount retained follows automatically.

In almost all firms, the explicit policy is to pay dividends which reflect increased profitability and rise fairly evenly in time, with a bottom line of dividends which match the rate of inflation. There is however some difference of emphasis and one or two exceptions.

In one family firm while it is policy at least to match inflation, dividends are kept low after that priority in order to retain funds for reinvestment. The shareholders, it was said, obtained their return by an increase in the value of the shares. In another firm it was admitted that dividend policy was geared to family requirements. A non-family-owned company had a policy of a stable dividend (taking account of inflation) coupled with a policy of keeping the dividend covered between two and two-and-a-half times. Another company with no dominant shareholders gave as one of its main objectives to pay a high return on shareholders capital. It commented that 'now that this policy is appreciated in the stock market it is very difficult to reduce the dividend and the need to maintain a high level of payout is reinforced'.

The statements made on the determinants of the dividend decision in the companion volume (pp. 69–70) were largely confirmed by the interviews with contractors but some points were not mentioned as important. Comments on them are as shown in Table 4.3 below.

4.6 PROFITABILITY AND RISK

An important theme running through all discussions on financial policy and profit-maximisation was the concern with risk, for risk-taking in contracting with its low assets has a more direct impact on the company's performance than in other industries. As is mentioned in Chapter 7 one loss-making project may have dire consequences for a firm in terms of negative cash-generation and on overall profits.

It may be for this reason that family-controlled firms appeared on the whole to be more risk-averse than 'non-family' companies. It was recognised that in addition to a more conservative attitude to risk which could be equated to lower profit expectations, two other disadvantages could arise from the sense of security generated by a family-owned business, where predators are not welcome and where there is a policy of not borrowing money from the market. The first is the lack of incentive to ensure efficiency in all aspects of the business where the pressure arising from the threat of predators does not arise. The second is that where firms are able to finance projects internally, this may lead to failure to ensure that the internal costs are properly compared with and assessed against the equivalent costs in the market-place. While the first feature is likely to be met mainly in a family-owned business, the second could be met in any type of firm

Table 4.3 Comparison of theoretical statements with comments from contractors interviewed

Statements	Comments
1. The firm's long-run dividend policy has to mirror that typical for the industry	Not specifically mentioned but implied in emphasis on keeping the stock market and institutional shareholders happy
2. If earnings grow dividends will increase	Generally true though one family firm aimed to have high retentions
3. Widely fluctuating earnings make managers reluctant to increase dividends for fear of not being able to maintain the increase	True; several firms stressed importance of dividends rising steadily or keeping up with inflation
4. Managers tend to prefer retained earnings as a source of funds especially in large firms	True but takes second place to other factors of 1. and 2. above
5. Shareholders will accept a lower dividend if the yield on new investment is high leading to expected capital gains	Not relevant to contracting but is to construction; not specifically stated for other businesses
6. Cost of external sources of funds will affect policy on dividends and retained earnings	Not discussed; this may be so but other factors override it so that the effect is small
7. The ability of managers to retain more profits than shareholders would like depends on their power which is related to share-ownership dispersion	True; however, a family-controlled firm had the strongest retention policy
8. Relationship between dividends and inflation cannot be predicted	Relationship between dividends and profits cannot be predicted. If profits are there then policy is that dividends should keep pace with inflation
9. Creditors insist on limits to the amount paid out in dividends	Few instances of this; pressure to maintain level of dividends where family relies on it may temper this position.

although its occurrence is obviously more likely in a firm which has not been exposed to the rigours of external finance-raising.

The positive aspects of cash-generation from contracting activities were set against the relatively low profits on turnover and in at least one company reference was made to the aim of achieving a somewhat different balance of businesses, that is, increasing the diversified elements of the business relative to contracting. It is obvious that this discussion could not take place where the construction firm was the subsidiary of a corporate firm.

4.7 RELATIONSHIPS WITH STOCKBROKERS

Firms visited relied on the services of more than one stockbroking firm to market their shares and regularly invited analysts from major city firms to visit them and discuss with a small group of directors (including of course the finance director) the affairs of the companies, insofar as the latter were prepared to do so! These visits would be arranged to coincide with or to follow shortly the announcement of half-yearly or annual results or at some other time when the companies wished to report on a new major development or acquisition or publicise a new venture. Major institutional shareholders would also be given the opportunity to discuss firms' strategies.

These contacts are important because the view taken of the company by shareholders and market analysis can affect the share price, the ability to raise capital and the likelihood of takeover bids. One contractor said that he had a policy of keeping well-in with the City:

> We have a number of institutional shareholders of whom none own in excess of 5 per cent and we listen carefully to the views of three or four major shareholders. This also has the advantage that if we keep them informed these shareholders have inside knowledge which they cannot use to their own personal advantage. We also have meetings with ten or twelve broker firms. We make sure that the City is supportive of our activities.

(The more relevant chapter in the Companion volume is Chapter 5; see Appendix in this volume).

NOTE AND REFERENCE

1. Cannon, J. and Hillebrandt, P.M. 'Financial Strategy' in Hillebrandt, P.M. and Cannon, J. (eds) *The Management of Construction Firms: Aspects of Theory* (London: Macmillan, 1989) Chapter 5. This source is often quoted and is indicated simply by page numbers or section numbers.

Part III
Implementation of Strategy

5 Marketing and Bidding Policy

5.1 MARKETING POLICY

The construction industry has been very slow to recognise the advantages of marketing as a tool to improve performance either in terms of market shares, level of sales or profitability. The main reason for the slowness stems from the fact that for a very long period post-war – indeed up to 1973 – the workload on the industry rose gradually so that the industry was never really short of work in spite of the complaints about stop/go. In fact there was a sellers' market. Another reason was that the major clients were in the public sector.

Contractors' major marketing effort was therefore not directed towards seeking work in a particular market area or from a certain client or group of clients, but towards getting on the tender list for construction work for central government, local authorities and nationalised industries. Their marketing behaviour towards the public-sector client was replicated where private clients were concerned. There was thus no need for them to put any effort into sophisticated marketing of their products since once on the tender list the dominant decision factor was that of price. Nor did they see the need to apply marketing techniques to increase their workload for the private sector.

Two quite separate changes in their environment led them to introduce marketing into policy-making. The first was the opening up of Middle East markets in the 1970s. Those companies determined to take the opportunities on offer had to tailor their marketing approach to the scale of private funds available as well as to the scale and glamour of some of the projects.

Second, when faced with a domestic recession brought about by a fall in demand from the private sector while the level of orders from the public sector was still declining, they became fully aware that the only means to overcome their unfavourable prospects was to strengthen their marketing efforts considerably.

Marketing, however, remains a less-well-developed activity than it is in large companies in other industries. In most companies there was a strong awareness that marketing policy had been the Cinderella of their range of activities and that there was a need to put more effort and resources into the development of a marketing policy than had been the case until quite recently. 'Marketing strategies are medium-term and if they are right they generate profits.' Marketing activities were being developed in a largely *ad hoc* manner. In only one company had consultants recently been employed to help to improve the marketing functions. No company was totally satisfied with its marketing.

Marketing was better integrated and had a more important role in companies which had diversified into the manufacture or distribution of products which require a strong marketing input or which were subsidiaries of corporations which were already fully aware of the importance of marketing.

Three separate aspects of marketing policy were discussed during the visits to the companies. They were market selection, market research and marketing sales.

5.1.1 Market selection

The determination of what broad markets the company group as a whole wishes to operate in is part of the overall strategy of the firm and is covered in our companion book in broad terms by Ramsay and described in this book in Chapters 2 and 3. However, the process of selecting markets does not stop at the main board level. Once the broad market areas are determined it is still a matter for the individual operating unit to decide on what sectors of that market it wishes to concentrate its activities. 'Operating companies are expected to find their own growth areas.' Indeed in many companies there were continual discussions at several levels as to the parts of the market in which they had a particular expertise and those which they might consider entering or leaving.

5.1.2 Market research

Both market research and the actual selling function are concerned with the implementation of the policy of determining what markets to be in. However the link between market selection on the one hand and market research and sales on the other was tenuous in a number of firms. In one instance a marketing director (not a main board director) had not seen the corporate plan though he had been in office some months. In many other companies market research and sales are seen as distinct activities and this is almost certainly damaging to both.

Most companies have someone in head office who is overseeing the marketing operations and is responsible for some sort of central market research. In some cases he looks at a particular segment of the market and examines its potential. In other cases it is a commercial information department which passes on pieces of information but does little analysis. In a few companies market research is linked to the consideration of new ideas for development which are really part of the determination of which markets to be in. In one or two companies it is also connected to the part of the organisation concerned with the funding of projects. In those companies where marketing was a well-integrated function, particular efforts were being devoted to the search for infrastructure projects which lent themselves to private funding and where public action seemed unlikely within the foreseeable future.

Quite apart from this type of market-data analysis, senior managers kept themselves informed through reading the trade press and through informal conversations within the company.

5.1.3 Marketing sales

The third element of marketing policy was sales marketing which in a number of companies had only recently become a formal part of their organisation. It included both a proactive approach, seeking clients before they have a definite project in mind and a reactive one, where the company responds formally to a specific demand situation.

Selling is a complex business in the construction industry partly due to the uniqueness of the product, but also to the fact that it is inherently difficult to locate and influence each prospective client, especially in the market for industrial building where there is a multitude of owners. In the commercial sector there is a relatively small number of very large development companies and a limited number of property agents and architects who operate in this market sector and marketing efforts can thus be better targeted than for industrial buildings. In this respect, the campaign led by the National Economic Development Office (NEDO) 'Thinking about Building' was a very worthwhile attempt to reach the industry's potential customers, in a situation where it would be excessively expensive for an individual company to do so.

One of the components of sales marketing is the projection of an image to clients of what the company represents: reliability, value for money, professional competence, integrity or innovative ideas were some examples given.

Both quality and reliability in construction depend on the managerial input, and because the product is unique, a company cannot establish standards of performance which can be guaranteed in the way in which those of assembly-type industries can be, where standards are those which the relevant machinery or plant is capable of meeting.

It is interesting that in different types of business in the same company both the image which is desired and the marketing approach are quite different. One company, for example, goes for volume and very tight pricing in one region but for quality assurance in another where they are able to obtain more work by negotiation. 'Thus these [areas] . . . are quite different in their approach to the source of their work, to the type of work and in the profit margins which they obtain. Each one is tailored to the specific market of the region.'

In one company, the marketing function was interpreted largely in terms of encouraging regions to maintain and improve contacts with local authority and regional offices of nationalised industries (the source of civil engineering work and public-sector building) and private architects (for private-sector construction). In those companies whose strength had for many years been that of its civil engineering division and where the public client was the near-unique source of work, it appeared especially difficult for senior managers with civil engineering background to recognise the importance of a marketing input to the company's strategic planning.

The differences between regions also sometimes dictate where the regional offices should be located. One contractor pointed out the importance of local feeling in this respect and its effect on obtaining work 'The problem of national identity in Scotland makes a separate company there very desirable and . . . the national and local feeling is so strong in Wales that there is a danger that a Cardiff-based firm may be excluded from work in Swansea.'

5.1.4 Location and integration of marketing function in the organisation

The difficulties met by companies in their attempts to develop and integrate their marketing policy into their strategic planning and to accommodate their marketing activities into their organisational framework were commented upon by both marketing managers and senior managers in other parts of companies.

In several companies, marketing was seen as an extension of, or part of, the responsibilities of operations managers or other specialists rather than as an independent function and this was indeed the traditional way. In most companies it was now recognised as a separate function but this was a recent development. About three-quarters of the companies visited now had some person or persons at head office in charge of what was called marketing. However, the practice varied considerably. In some cases this person was really trying to develop a proper marketing role including encouraging others in the subsidiaries to change their attitudes. In other instances what was called marketing was really publicity and the promotion of the company image.

It is probably mainly because marketing as a service to enhance performance has only very recently been introduced in a number of companies that it appears to be relatively poorly integrated and organised. In one company, everyone from the chairman down – including managers, subsidiary companies, project finance managers, regional staff and estimators – was expected to do some marketing, though there was also a full-time marketing staff in that company. There is no disadvantage in asking that personnel should take any reasonable opportunity to promote the company. However, it is not and cannot be a substitute for a disciplined planned and continuous marketing operation by someone who is charged with the responsibility for this task.

It is easy to undertand the dichotomy faced by those large companies when trying to establish an effective marketing function. On the one hand marketing can be defined as a service to the various activities of those companies and in this case it makes organisational sense to provide for it at head office where other services are centralised. On the other hand the fixed location of the product of construction firms favours siting the marketing role where the product is developed which is at the level of the region.

Thus there was no company where the marketing function was fully centralised. It was sometimes located only in regions. Nowhere was it suggested that marketing should be divorced from regional activities. The pace of change is great at the moment as indicated below:

As with all activities of the group the subsidiary companies and divisions have their own organisation for undertaking specialist activities and most of the marketing is done by the subsidiary companies. There are some trends away from this: for example, the regional contracting organisation which has just been set up, will have its own marketing director so that some direction of marketing operations will be brought into head office.

Until recently marketing was always undertaken in the building and civil engineering operations by the regional subsidiary companies and not at a total group level. However a marketing manager for all building and civil engineering operations has now been appointed and the marketing managers in each subsidiary company report to him.

There is often now a dual reporting system for the regional marketing managers. Regional marketing staff report to both the managing director and the senior marketing manager at head office. In a number of instances marketing staff could be described as part-time in the sense that marketing is part of the responsibilities undertaken by field regional managers. Indeed at the regional level the responsibility for marketing is unclear in a number of cases.

The vast range in the scale of projects which the companies are able to carry out led to further difficulties in allocating marketing responsibilities. The larger the scale of a project to be marketed, the less likely the involvement of the marketing staff as the matter would then be handled by the managing director of the relevant division or of the company itself. This is quite different from the situation which is met, for instance, in companies in food manufacturing where the marketing and sales function has a formal hierarchical structure, and where marketing responsibilities are divided up according to type of product and size of customer. Senior staff control the whole of the marketing activity and personally handle the largest accounts.

The importance of personal relationships in marketing was highlighted in one company which insisted that where an existing client with a project in one region wanted a new development in another region, all dealings with him would be handled by the region involved in the earlier project.

5.1.5 Background of marketing personnel and their acquaintance with theory

Most persons concerned with sales had a background of work in construction especially if they were employed in a subsidiary company or in the regional organisation.

Those persons at head office responsible for marketing were sometimes construction managers who had been given this special responsibility and were sometimes recruited from outside, often from manufacturing industry or in one case from a firm of management consultants. Where they were recruited from outside they had some awareness of the theory on the selection of markets as highlighted by Ramsay in our companion volume. Where they were recruited from within the organisation their theoretical knowledge was slight and had been derived from short courses.

One person who had recently been put in charge of the development of a marketing strategy confessed that when given this responsibility he did not know what marketing was. He understood what selling was and his firm's selling policy had been based on their past performance and their price, which was satisfactory if they had customers at their door but they no longer had. He spent some time going round the parts of the company in the UK and then went to the USA to try to understand how certain things happened there and what their impact was. Then he had a two-day course at Cranfield and suddenly, during that course, the whole understanding of marketing emerged. He understood that what he was selling was a product, even though it was not something which could be picked up and handled. He understood about product launches and pricing and distribution. He was fascinated by the very simple matrix of the markets divided into 'cats', 'dogs', 'cows', and 'stars'. He was then able to define what products his company was actually selling.

(The cats and dogs matrix is illustrated in Figure 2.2 in Ramsay's chapter in the companion volume and explained here in Chapter 2.)[1]

5.2 BIDDING POLICIES

There are a number of different contractual arrangements between client and contractor. Flanagan and Norman in the chapter on pricing policy in the companion book distinguish eleven types as follows:

1. Design – build (package deal, turnkey)
2. Design/bid with contractor competing part of the design/build
3. Lump sum, fixed price
4. Lump sum, fluctuating price
5. Schedule of rates, remeasured on completion
6. Management fee contracting with guaranteed maximum price and a fixed management fee
7. Management fee contracting with a target price and a fixed management fee
8. Management fee contracting with a target price and a fluctuating management fee
9. Cost reimbursement
10. Construction management with separate trade contracts (contractor or professional consultant) with trades bid upon a fixed lump sum
11. Construction management with separate trade contracts, with trades on cost reimbursement (p. 130).[2]

They go on to say:

so far as price determination is concerned, two distinguishing features of the contractual arrangements are important:

(i) the selection and number of contractors competing for the particular project;
(ii) whether the initially quoted price can be negotiated between client and contractor prior to the final award of the contract.

These features allow the construction of the matrix in Figure 9.1 in which is illustrated the economic model appropriate to the particular combination of features and typical forms of contract to which they apply (p. 130).

The most relevant models for the building industry are *A*, *B* and *D* in Figure 5.1 (9.1 in the companion volume). It is highly unlikely that a client would call for a bid from a single contractor without the option of subsequent negotiation. About the only situation in which this is likely to arise is where contractor and client belong to the same

NEGOTIATION

		Yes	No
		Bilateral/ A **Contestable** **Monopoly** negotiated tender with single contractor	**(Contestable)** C **Monopoly** contractor within same group
Number of competing contractors	*One*		
	Several	**Auction** B **with** **Rebid** negotiated competitive tender; two stage tender	**Sealed** D **Bid** **Auction** competitive tender; lump sum bid

Figure 5.1   Economic models and building contracts

Source: Flanagan, R. and Norman, G., 'Pricing Policy' in Hillebrandt, P.M. and Cannon, J. (eds) *The Management of Large Construction Firms: Aspects of Theory* (London: Macmillan, 1989) Figure 9.1.

organisation, e.g. where contractor and developer are subsidiaries of the same corporation (see *C* in Figure 5.1).

Flanagan and Norman concentrate their analysis on competitive tenders without negotiation and on negotiation. Whatever the contractual arrangements however the first decision by the contractor is whether to bid or not.

5.2.1   The decision to bid

Generally decisions on what projects to bid for are taken at the operating unit level though several companies have limits on the authority of their managers in each operating unit so that for larger contracts or contractor where it is judged that the risks are great a board member or even the Managing Director or Executive Board may be involved in the required decisions. In one company it was said that 'Normally the individual parts of the organisation determine their tendering policy themselves but if the regions, for example, need help on onerous tender or contract conditions they can obtain advice from the legal department.'

Reasons why firms might decide not to bid included:

1. company lacks the skills to undertake it;
2. unsatisfactory payment arrangement especially for work abroad, e.g. payment in non-convertible currencies;
3. too many competitors – six seemed to be regarded as reasonable maximum;
4. inadequate capacity in the estimating department;
5. unsatisfactory experience in a particular area, e.g. difficult trade union sector.

Managers look at the information available in relation to the business. They consider for each project the level of competition and are unlikely to bid if there are more than six firms involved. They look at their ability to resource the project and they look at the impact on the forward trading. Timing is exceedingly important, that is to say they plan their turnover.

Less important reasons often covered by the bid price rather than in refusing the invitation to bid were:

1. unsatisfactory past experiences with client or designer in personality or payment;
2. high cost;
3. inadequate information.

A few companies were asked about the way in which they handled the situation when they had been invited to tender but did not wish to do so: 'If we let the client know soon enough that we wish to withdraw there are no problems. We do not put in high prices to avoid getting the job because that is more likely than withdrawals to result in our not being asked next time.' Another company said that it did not put in cover prices but that other contractors sometimes did.

5.2.2 Determining the bid price

In actually determining the bid price companies started with the estimated costs and then took into consideration the scope of the work, the likely risk, the likely competitors and the volume of work in the hands of the competitors, their volume of work on hand, the influence of the project on the future workload and their ability to provide all necessary resources for the project. Thus they were considering not only the money estimated cost, but also, in effect, the opportunity cost of undertaking the project and the chances of obtaining it against various competitors as suggested by the theory.

> In identifying the optimal mark-up it must be recognised that contractors do not have unlimited resources nor do they tender on only single contracts. Winning a particular contract will carry implications for the resources available to undertake future contracts. In economic terms, the contractor in formulating a bid for any one contract must, therefore, take into account both the direct costs and the opportunity costs of the contract (p. 133, reference number altered).[3]

Contractors' mark-ups would be higher if they had a lot of work because they could afford not to win the contract and also if their competitors had a lot of work because their competitors would probably put in high bids too.

Contractors generally had a fairly good idea from the grape-vine who their competitors would be on any project, though this is not public information. They also knew roughly how their competitors' order books stood and how they had been bidding on previous projects. Some companies kept detailed records of this information; others relied on the memory and knowledge of their managers. No company used any computer programmes to determine bid price, though they did use computers to help in the preparation of estimates.

One company explained as follows:

> We keep detailed analyses of competitors' bids because we must know how well they are doing in relation to the total market. We do not make any calculations on a model basis of their competitive position for any contract because managers *know* the competition and no calculation is necessary. The regional manager will wish to know that the jobs obtained are not being obtained by too large a margin. Our bid should be within 2 per cent of the next bid. The worst possible situation is to obtain work too cheaply.

An important element in the price-determination process was the estimated risk. These are of several types:

1. errors by the company itself, for example, a mistake in estimating or poor management;
2. difficulties arising with other parties to the process;
3. technical risks of the job, for example, ground conditions;
4. financial risks of the job, for example, not being paid or being unable to bring money from abroad to the UK;
5. onerous contract conditions;
6. the employment of unsuitable subcontractors or – in the case of subcontractors – working for an inefficient main contractor (including the danger that he goes into liquidation).

Should they occur, some of the losses arising from these situations may be recouped by claims. Indeed risks of this type are sometimes even welcomed because they can lead to a beneficial claim situation, though other companies stressed that they preferred a smoothly running project to beneficial claims which presumably themselves have substantial direct and opportunity costs.

These risks bear little relation to the size of contract so that it is difficult to put a percentage on to the mark-up for them. On the other hand in general a company which has a large number of smaller projects is likely to be subject to less risk overall than a company of similar size with a few large contracts.

The theoretical analysis on tendering undertaken by Flanagan and Norman brings them to some general conclusions:

The highly simplified analysis . . . leads to rather more general conclusions. First, a tender list that is drawn up without attention being paid to the relative efficiencies and experience of the contractors is likely to lead to the client paying a higher price. In addition, there is at least some possibility that the contract will be won by a relatively inefficient and inexperienced contractor. Finally, note that . . . inefficient contractor applied a relatively low mark-up. If such a contractor wins the tender competition the client is exposed to greater risk. These conclusions lead to the further implication that pre-tender interviews with potential contractors are likely to generate more competitive prices and reduce the risk-exposure of the client. These interviews will obviate problems that will arise in selecting an experienced contractor or one who has a heavy current workload (pp. 135–6).

Contractors would find these conclusions in keeping with their own, sometimes bitter, experience.

There was little discussion with contractors on the way in which a negotiated price is reached though some of the 'flavour' of negotiations did come out in the discussion:

Negotiation is normally undertaken for old clients on a formula basis, often at prime cost with an open-book situation. The figure for the overhead component of cost is supported from the company accounts and a reasonable profit is added. One of the secrets of successful negotiation is to know the person with whom you are negotiating, his problems and where potential difficulties lie. Clients react well to a position where the contractor is aware of their requirements.

Flanagan and Norman discussed negotiation in some detail and it is so interesting that it is worth reproducing much of it here. Its relevance is clear.

An increasing proportion of building contracts is awarded on the basis of negotiation at some stage between client and contractor . . .

The process of *negotiation* itself warrants attention as a determinant of the final contract price. Effectively there is now a bilateral monopoly (Box A in Figure 5.1): a single buyer (the client) facing a single seller (the selected contractor). Both will have identified a price range within which they are willing to negotiate. For the client the upper limit of this range is determined by the benefits (evaluated in some financial terms) [which] the building is expected to generate and an evaluation of the worth of the managerial services the contractor is expected to provide. The lower limit is much less precise, relating to what is felt by the client to be the minimum price the contractor is likely to accept while still providing a satisfactory service.

For the contractor the lower limit is determined by his evaluation of the costs (direct and opportunity) he will incur and the risks he will have to accept. The upper limit is a more subjective estimate of what he feels the client would be willing to pay rather than pull out of the contract or enter into negotiation with another contractor.

The potential for an equilibrium price being identified depends upon the extent to which these two price ranges overlap . . .

There remains the question, of course, of where the equilibrium price will fall. No definitive answer is possible, the outcome being dependent upon the distribution of knowledge, risk and power between the participants in the negotiation: client and contractor. Some qualitative statements can, however, be made. The appropriate economic model, as noted above, is bilateral monopoly. From the client's perspective the desire is for a low price consistent with the project being completed on time, to specification and with the minimum of contractual claims. His power in the negotiation will be determined by the quality of professional advice he receives, his own experience as a client of the building industry and, by implication, whether the project under consideration is 'one-off' or part of a regular building programme.

From the contractor's perspective, the desire is to find a competitive price that is consistent with an acceptable rate of return, given the risk and uncertainties inherent in the construction process. Again a distinction has to be drawn between 'one-off' and regular clients of the industry. In addition, and related to this, the contractor must take into account the extent to which the client has committed himself to a single contractor. The less experienced the client, the more he is committed to the contractor, and the poorer his professional advice, the greater is the relative power of the contractor.

The lower the degree to which the client is committed, and the more frequently the client commissions building work, the more relevant economic model shades from bilateral monopoly into a contestable market – and a contestable monopoly.[4]

The essential feature of contestable markets is that there exist potential suppliers of that market who can enter *and leave* the market relatively costlessly. If too high a price is charged by incumbent firms a potential entrant will come in, undercut the incumbents and so take part of the market, then leave once price has been competed down. Any incumbent firm is, therefore, severely constrained in its pricing policy by the threat of such *potential* entry.

These principles can be applied to building contracts allocated by tender and subsequent negotiation. Those invited to tender incur costs in preparation of the tender documents, but these costs are a relatively small proportion of total costs on a new project, and can be treated as sunk costs on an existing project. In other words, entry to and exit from negotiation is relatively costless. Thus, while the selected contractor is effectively in a monopoly position at the negotiation stage in that he faces no competition from other contractors *within* the negotiation, he does face potential competition from other contractors in two ways if he pushes for too high a price. First, the client may decide to withdraw from the negotiation and appoint another contractor. Second, the client may choose not to appoint this contractor on future projects, but rather to go to one of his competitors.

This does not imply that experienced clients will always negotiate the lowest prices. Rather, it implies that they should obtain a more favourable combination of price, delivery and other more subjective measures of quality (pp. 136–9, reference number changed).

(The most relevant chapters in the companion volume are 2 and 9; see Appendix in this volume.)

NOTES AND REFERENCES

1. Ramsay, W., 'Business Objectives and Strategy' in Hillebrandt, P.M. and Cannon, J. (eds) *The Management of Construction Firms: Aspects of Theory* (London: Macmillan, 1989).
2. Flanagan, R. and Norman, G., 'Pricing Policy' in Hillebrandt, P.M. and Cannon, J. (eds) *The Management of Construction Firms: Aspects of Theory* (London: Macmillan, 1989). This source is often quoted and is indicated simply by page numbers.
3. Opportunity cost is the cost of the loss of the opportunity to use resources elsewhere – in this case to undertake a different contract.
4. See Baumol, W.J., 'Contestable Markets: An Uprising in the Theory of Industry Structure', *American Economic Review*, vol. 71 (1982) pp. 1–15.

6 International Policy

This chapter concentrates on contracting operations abroad by UK construction firms. Their operations in other businesses abroad are an aspect of diversification and are referred to in Chapter 3.

6.1 OVERSEAS OPERATIONS

Virtually all the firms in the survey have operations overseas, though not necessarily in contracting. All had at some time acted as main contractors or subcontractors abroad. However, there has been a substantial change in the past ten years or so in the types of businesses in which they are working outside the UK. They have been replaced by property development, housing, building materials production and by some businesses such as coal- and mineral-mining and instrument manufacture, which are almost completely unconnected with construction.

There has also been a substantial change in the geographical areas of operation. Whereas ten and certainly twenty years ago the area of operation was very widespread, because contractors were undertaking projects anywhere in the world, the shift towards manufacture or mining which are located in a specific country has meant less-widely dispersed activity. There was also more geographical specialisation in contracting operations, though by the time the interviews were conducted the dominant position formerly held by the Middle East had declined. Indeed the fortunes of UK contractors have followed more or less the absolute values of the work done as well as its geographical location as shown in Table 6.1 – not surprising in view of the fact that about twenty contractors probably account for over three-quarters of the work done abroad.

6.2 CHANGES IN THE MARKET FOR CONTRACTING WORK OVERSEAS

The principal reason for the change in the work done abroad by UK firms is the change in the total market situation both on the demand

Table 6.1 Value of construction work by British firms overseas 1982/83 and 1987 – £million (current prices)

Location	1982/83[b]	1987[b]
European Community[a]	24	83
Rest of Europe	80	32
Middle East in Asia	669	222
Middle East in Africa	62	55
Rest of Asia	264	179
Rest of Africa	524	205
Americas	436	672
Oceania	255	248
All countries	2314	1696

Notes: [a]Prior to 1985/86 figures for Greece, Portugal and Spain were included in the rest of Europe.
[b]1982/83 financial year, 1987 calendar year.
Source: Department of the Environment, *Housing and Construction Statistics 1977–87* (HMSO, 1988) Table 1.1.

side and the supply side, and contractors were keen to elaborate on these changes. It was generally thought that the demand world-wide had fallen considerably over say the past ten years, first because of the fall in oil revenues, which had been used to finance construction projects, and second because of a decline in aid from international agencies for construction projects.

On the supply side there has been an increase in the capability of local contractors to carry out work. Contractors stressed the very great increase in competition from developing or newly industrialised countries all over the world and from Eastern European countries. Contractors from these countries tend to have lower wages and salaries and less experience than contractors from USA or Western Europe.

Moreover, some contractors from developing and newly industrialised countries are backed by governments whose aim is not so much to make a profit as to obtain hard currency or equipment. Thus, as a deliberate policy, they go in to the tender with a price which is below cost. In these circumstances it is hardly surprising that margins have fallen and that UK contractors see their effective market as having fallen even more than the total world market for expatriate contractors.

6.3   UK CONTRACTORS' ADVANTAGES IN THE WORLD MARKET

In the companion volume, Howard Seymour divided the comparative advantages of firms operating internationally into those which were specific to the country and those specific to the firm.[1] The country-specific advantages may be considered in terms of

(a) the special assets of UK contractors;
(b) government support;
(c) the legal framework;
(d) the reputation of professionals.

Because the industry is very management-intensive, the assets of UK contractors are its managers, rather than some specific technology or fixed assets as in other industries. The experience of UK contractors in large complex projects, especially in civil engineering, was outstanding in the immediate post-war period and matched only in certain areas by a few countries. The UK expertise may well be as good as before or even better, but the number of countries which can produce such an asset has increased so that the comparative advantage of the UK has decreased. A few companies suggested however that the comparative advantage of the UK was that her managers were paid less than US and European senior managers.

It is interesting that the comparative advantage of a number of countries which have entered the international contracting market was seen to lie in very different factors, notably the ability to provide large amounts of cheap labour together with supervisors. With a few notable exceptions it is a common complaint by the contractors that they receive too little support from government compared with that given to competitors from other countries. The support given to some developing countries' contractors to enable them to earn hard currency and obtain plant (which can only be bought with hard currency) has already been mentioned in Section 6.2 above. This means that the governments are subsidising the contracting firms, some of which are in any case government-owned. The UK contractors were not of course expecting any support at this level.

They did, however, feel that they had a reasonable case for British government officials and Ministers to give more support in terms of information and political backing in obtaining contracts abroad. The assistance from diplomatic posts was described as 'non-existent or minor'. It had been found that commercial counsellors in Embassies often regarded their appointment as a stepping-stone to higher diplomatic posts and had little interest in commercial work. One contractor felt that there had been an improvement recently. Furthermore, a contractor said that whereas it was common practice in France for Ministers to give all possible support to French contractors in obtaining contracts, including several visits to the country in question, in England this is rare. The involvement of Overseas Development Administration was said to be very important but little was said of the role of the Department of Trade and Industry or the Department of the Environment, as the ministry dealing with construction.

The Prime Minister was seen as having done more to help to obtain construction work abroad than most other ministers though often not enough. Her intervention is of course for the mammoth projects only; support at the appropriate levels for all sizes of projects is what is required. One contractor was seconding a very senior person to the Department of Trade and Industry which it was hoped would allow him to understand how government operates in this area. In some cases where government might in principle be willing to give backing, support is in fact not available because government refuses to back an individual firm when there is more than one UK contractor bidding for a project. It was suggested that this could be done on a first-come, first-served basis.

There was considerable criticism of the way in which ECGD insurance and certain grants are administered. Several contractors said that many of their European competitors and others too received considerably more favourable terms for guarantees and insurance cover. It was considered by some that even with the same amount of money available the financial and contractual guarantees would be better administered in the hands of a bank rather than by the Treasury and the ECGD. While it is accepted that the risks of working abroad are high and therefore that the cost of insurance would be high, it was pointed out by some that the costs were now so heavy that it was not possible to have ECGD insurance for the risky projects without pricing oneself out of the market and where the risks were less substantial it was more advantageous for the contractor to carry the risk himself than to pay the high premiums required. It was considered that the main benefit of guarantees and insurance from the government sector was for projects which were funded as part of the package.

The failure of the government to give any financial help in funding the Bosporus Bridge which stimulated questions in the House of Commons may in the long run lead to more sympathetic treatment of UK contractors. The old question of tied aid was raised, with contractors pointing out the advantages enjoyed by US firms since USAID loans are tied to US contractors. While UK contractors may have some advantages with UK aid, firms from other countries are not excluded from tendering. Moreover it was acknowledged that the scale of US aid had been large compared with UK aid.

Overall the view was that government help for contractors was less than in many other countries and that therefore in this respect there was a comparative disadvantage, not an advantage to UK contractors.

In the companion volume Seymour drew the conclusion that:

The UK government should assist UK contractors by providing a larger budget for mixed credit and tied aid components of export credit deals, by encouraging more use of Commonwealth links and matching other countries' support measures. It would also help to foster greater cooperation and less competition amongst UK contractors in work abroad (p. 54).

One respect in which the UK does have an advantage over some other countries is that much of the legal framework, contractual arrangements, building regulations and specifications across the world and especially in former British Territories are based on those in Britain and are therefore familiar to British contractors making it easier to meet various requirements. Similar advantages accrue to the French in territories where they had colonies or influence.

Lastly, contractors mentioned that the UK has the advantage that its consulting engineers are highly regarded and this is of some assistance to British contractors over and above their familiarity with the specifications of British consultants. This advantage, while undoubtedly positive, may be overstated. One of the reasons for the high regard for British consultants is their independence and integrity. They cannot afford to recommend British contractors unless they regard them as very well qualified to undertake the work.

One of the policy implications of Seymour's analysis was that 'They [contractors] should also bring their successful performance to the attention of UK consultants so that the latter may utilise UK contractors without abandoning their impartial advice to clients' (p. 54). This is more a matter for the individual firms than for the industry. It would be expected that contractors would ensure that UK consulting engineers were well aware of their successful projects, though this point was not specifically discussed.

6.4 ADVANTAGES SPECIFIC TO INDIVIDUAL FIRMS

The advantages enjoyed by particular firms over other UK firms may be summarised as follows:

1. Any firm which has a large capital base has an advantage in obtaining contracts in that it is able to convince the client that it has the resources to complete the contract and to carry any risk. When the contract is linked to some financial package this is even more important. Some UK contractors cited this advantage as one of the reasons why they regarded it as desirable to acquire some other company, preferably one with a larger asset base. The number of companies which on their own have a sufficiently large capital base is limited.
2. Similarly only a large firm is able to carry the substantial risks of working abroad. (Even if the contract is covered by an ECGD guarantee, this only covers a part of the total risk). Nevertheless, several companies said that they put an absolute limit on the size of contract which they would undertake alone, £50–70 million in one case, though it was pointed out that the risk is not necessarily proportional to the size of the job. Beyond the limit set the company would seek to undertake the project in a joint venture with another contractor.
3. Some firms have a specific advantage in that they are expert in a particular type of construction such as pipelines, outfalls, chemical engineering or the cleaning and purging of pipes.
4. Those firms who are able to mount financial packages or to engage in work with specific characteristics in terms of the contractual arrangements – for example, some types of management contracting – may be able to obtain an edge over their competitors.
5. It is interesting that the management structure of a company in the UK can give it an advantage or disadvantage in work abroad. Those companies which give their site agents and other managers a large amount of responsibility in running a project are more likely to be able to operate abroad than those where the site agent has a large back-up of central services and is closely supervised. This is also mentioned under section 6.6 below.

6.5   THE RESPONSE OF CONTRACTORS TO THE MARKET SITUATION AND THEIR COMPARATIVE ADVANTAGE

The first conclusion on policy from the chapter by Seymour in the companion volume was that 'An overall corporate strategy on overseas operations is of vital importance and it should be based on differentiation of products in overseas markets (p. 54).

It is apparent from what has already been said that the corporate strategy of a number of companies on overseas activities is in a state of flux. They had not all yet decided exactly how they would respond to the changes which developed in the 1980s.

A very few have withdrawn from overseas contracting operations and one or two are in the process of doing so or are considering it. The majority of contractors interviewed, however, had decided to keep a presence in some way or another in overseas markets. One wanted to increase turnover abroad from its previous low levels. Some contractors still regarded overseas activities as very important to them and were devoting effort to changing the way in which they operated rather than to the level of their operations.

Because of the changes in the market situation there has been a corresponding change in the types of contracting work abroad undertaken by construction firms. At one time the main component of their work abroad was one-off, very large, mainly civil engineering projects undertaken alone or as joint ventures anywhere abroad. Contractors now bid for such projects only if they have a very specific advantage or expertise. Furthermore they do not bid for projects which have very long tender lists. Few will bid if there are more than ten contractors and a maximum of about six is regarded as a reasonable number. This means that the projects funded by the World Bank with about forty on the list are now rarely bid for by British contractors. The Overseas Development Administration usually limits the number to six to eight contractors. Other development funds – e.g. the European Development Fund and the United Nations Development Programme – limit the lists but they are still fairly long. In determining whether to bid or not, the nationality of other contractors on the list is important. UK contractors are happy to compete against European or North American companies, but cannot compete against countries which have quite different standards and costs.

The alternative type of operation is that concentrated on a particular area of the world. Several contractors have reduced the number of areas in which they operate, remaining in those areas where they have special connections, though also looking at areas which they believe to have potential for operations on a long-term basis. It is interesting that several companies are operating in Africa, for example, West Africa, Southern Africa, excluding South Africa itself, and East Africa. In part this is because they have long-standing connections there but also because the competition has been less, though the numerous contractors of various nationalities who have been working in the Middle East are now seeking work elsewhere including Africa so that this situation may no longer hold.

Contracting operations abroad have declined though in a few cases overseas work remains at around half their contracting turnover.

These two types of operation, one-off large projects and continuing activities in a certain territory, are described in theoretical terms, suitably interpreted for the special characteristics of construction, as exports and foreign direct investment respectively. It was stated by Seymour in the companion volume that:

> Exporting and FDI [Foreign Direct Investment] are differentiable by the length of time the firm's personnel are in a country. Where markets warrant a degree of FDI but experience fluctuating demand, the firm may 'top up' the local presence of personnel at times of high demand for the firm's services. A similar arrangement may also be made in high-risk, politically unstable areas where a continual local presence is required. In both cases the contractor will experience a more efficient use of resources and at the same time lessen risk (p. 51).

The conclusion from Seymour's work in this matter was that 'Ownership advantages must be relevant to the region where the firm chooses to operate and given the nature of the contractor's product, a combination of exporting and FDI in any one market may be beneficial' (p. 54). Some contractors operate in both types of market, but rarely in any one country at the same time.

A major factor in determining policy on overseas operations is the attitude to risk. It is generally accepted that profits are higher abroad than on work in the UK but that the risk is greater. Companies which in general are prepared to take risks become more risk-averse once they have experienced a substantial loss on any particular contract.

However, if contractors become more risk-averse, it is necessary in bidding to increase prices and this makes them less competitive. The risks in overseas contracts, many of which also apply to UK work may be listed as follows:

1. that the firms do bad work;
2. that they make a mistake in the tender price;
3. that they do not get paid;
4. that the relevant rates of exchange change;
5. that the conditions of contract are not right especially those concerning ground conditions. There could be unforeseen circumstances which are not covered by the contract and where the risk lies with the contractor;
6. that the labour is not available or not available at the price expected. This could arise from the letting of contracts for other work.

The only one of these risks covered by ECGD insurance is item 3. While it is a fact that all these risks apply also in the UK they are enhanced when working abroad because the environment is less familiar, control of a project is more difficult, the conditions of contract may be different and the chances of the client being able to avoid payment of all his dues are greater. Litigation is expensive and very time-consuming and judgements in some countries may not be unbiased.

Another feature of operations abroad now that the one-off large contact is getting more difficult to obtain on a profitable basis is the need to have a senior manager in a territory before work is obtained in order to obtain information and make contacts. As one contractor put it:

> In order to obtain work it is important to get into the information chain early. To some extent one can do that from the UK end but generally speaking it is necessary to have someone resident in the country where you are trying to obtain work, who is well-known and understands the local problems.

Most contractors accepted that in breaking into a new territory a long stay of a year or more by a representative of the company might be necessary before work was obtained. The cost of keeping a person abroad in these circumstances is about £100 000 a year. Costs of estimating may be two or three times those in the UK. Thus the decision to operate in an area in the longer term is one which involves considerable investment. This means that the size of the initial project needs to be, say, £5 million before the costs of working there begin to be covered. The first job can then be used as a springboard for further projects.

One of the ways to limit the risk to any one contractor in a large project abroad (or indeed in the UK) is to undertake it on a joint-venture basis with another contractor. Indeed several contractors had in mind an absolute limit on the size of project they would do on their own (see section 6.4, item 2 above).

The desirability of going into joint ventures with other contractors in developed countries is highlighted as one of the conclusions in the Seymour chapter. As the size of contracts increases so does the desirability of joint ventures. One contractor who has considerable experience in joint ventures with UK contractors said:

> In a joint venture the two contracting firms have a fully integrated management and this leads to a commercial success because the basic loyalties are to the joint venture itself. It is interesting that contractors are quite able to compete hard one day and joint-venture another. There are few problems of different methods of operation, which may mean that contractors' behaviour is becoming more alike.

Another company stressed the dangers of incompatibility of objectives of joint-venture partners especially from two different countries: 'In joint ventures one needs to make sure objectives are compatible with those of the partner. For instance, Japanese contractors are often willing to accept very low margins because they see low prices as the means of penetrating the market.'

In many countries a local partner is essential in obtaining work, for example, in the Middle East. Moreover in certain countries it is a legal requirement to have a local company in order to obtain work. It may also be necessary to have at least a 51 per cent indigenous shareholding in an expatriate's local firm. This raises the question of the circumstances in which a company would joint-venture with another in a developing country. The theory suggests that one of the major disadvantages of a joint venture is that the know-how may be passed on to the other firm involved. In many instances in developing countries where a local partner is required, this is not as dangerous a risk as might be thought because the local partner may not be a contracting firm at all but a more general business whose prime job is to make contacts and help to obtain the work. This was confirmed by the interviews.

UK contractors are differentiating their products in order to increase their comparative advantage in obtaining work abroad. They are exploring ways of changing the services they are offering in order to have an edge over their competitors. One of the main ways in which this is happening is the offer of a complete package to the client including the provision of finance. An increasing number of UK contractors are providing this type of service. It does mean however that more staff and very specialised staff are required at head office to negotiate finance with the city and set up the project. It follows that the turnover in this type of arrangement or the potential turnover has to be substantial to carry these overheads. This change is in keeping with Seymour's conclusion that 'Contractors should take advantage of the international expertise of UK manufacturing firms and of the London financial markets to generate demand for their services' (p. 54).

In some countries or groups of countries where contractors have had a presence for some time and are well-known, the locally based manager tries to identify a project which would be beneficial and convince the government to back it, perhaps helping to obtain international funding.

Yet another relatively recent development has been the offer of a management service for a fee or on a contract basis, in which the UK contractor essentially supervises the local contractors. At least one contractor has been negotiating with the World Bank on this type of project. Such projects are at least as likely as joint ventures to work the contractor out of a job because eventually the local contractors will learn enough to manage the total project themselves.

6.6   PERSONNEL FOR WORK ABROAD

In order to work satisfactorily abroad, a contractor must use a high calibre of manager who is prepared to take decisions without reference to head office, is willing to move, willing to train a subordinate to take over from him, communicates well with his boss in the UK, and is able to judge when he needs help and is willing to ask for it. This is necessary because there is no close supervision of his activities and because the range of functions which he has to fulfil are much greater than in the UK. Indeed, his activities are more like running a business than running a site. He will have to deal with government departments – on immigration for example; with Customs and Excise; with Port Authorities, and with all the professions involved in projects as well as with the clients. Even on site his responsibilities are much greater than in the UK where he will obtain help from head office service departments or will have people trained by them. He must also learn about the way people in the country operate, the legal framework and, indeed, the total environment. In addition if he is operating in remote areas, he will have to provide prefabricated living quarters for his workforce. The demands on him are very great. One contractor who was withdrawing from overseas work said that part of the reason for the difficulties was that the company did not have people of this calibre.

It is not surprising that successful managers operating abroad have gained experience and knowledge which it would have taken many more years to acquire in any other way. 'Those going abroad are often those with more personal drive and ambition than those who stay at home and they get experience which they might not get in the UK till ten or fifteen years later.' When they return to the UK they are often given senior management positions, though it may be difficult to place them at once. A few find it difficult to settle, and leave to go abroad again with another company.

The remuneration package for personnel abroad is expensive. Most companies which have substantial overseas operations have some rules for determining salaries, for example, UK rate plus country uplift. Several companies give assistance with school fees in the UK and other financial arrangements such as insurance, etc. Tours of duty vary greatly from one year for those with no family, up to long periods of five or six years. Beyond these periods it is felt that a manager should not remain in the same place because he becomes too involved in the local scene and is no longer independent.

Companies which have substantial operations abroad seem to have no difficulty in persuading people to take a tour overseas, presumably because they attract those interested in work abroad and recruit with that in mind. Some companies with a small proportion of work abroad also find no problems though others say that the short notice which they are able to give makes it difficult to find the right people to go. No company recruited from outside for its senior management positions abroad because, with the great responsibility their managers have to bear, they need tried and experienced people.

NOTE AND REFERENCE

1. Seymour, H., 'International Contracting' in Hillebrandt, P.M. and Cannon, J. (eds) *The Management of Construction Firms: Aspects of Theory* (London: Macmillan, 1989) Chapter 4. Several references are made to this source and are denoted simply by a page or section number.

7 Structure and Organisation

7.1 OWNERSHIP

Table 1.2 shows that of the top thirty-five firms with major building and civil engineering interests, excluding subsidiaries of conglomerates, seven were private limited companies. Among these firms, half were 'family-type' either in the sense that the combined family-related shareholdings of large shareholders effectively gives them financial control, or in the sense that a number of directors are members of the same family and hold management control. This is a quite remarkable situation, when compared with the ownership and control met in other industries.

The presence of a large number of family firms among the thirty-five largest construction firms is probably attributable to the positive cash flow and low capital base of contracting activities. This meant that there was no call on capital injections by the family, unlike the situation in manufacturing industry as that became more capital-intensive. Until those family-controlled construction firms adopted a policy of diversification, as has happened in the past decade, there was no requirement for new capital to enable them to grow.

It might be helpful to draw together the factors that differentiate the functioning of the family firms from others. The aspects which are important are:

1. it is difficult for a family firm to grow fast because it cannot easily raise capital without dilution of the family shareholding (see Chapter 3);
2. the same difficulty affects any diversification policy (see Chapter 3);
3. a family-owned firm may be less willing to retain profits for growth or to accept a fall in the income of the shareholders when the company profits fall on account of their dependence on the income from this source (see Chapter 4);
4. on the other hand a family-controlled firm does not have to worry over-much about the Stock Exchange valuation and is able to take a longer-term view of its opportunities (see Chapter 4);

5. a family firm which has a large number of members of the family
   in top management may lose other good managers because they
   cannot see prospects of promotion (see Chapter 8);
6. it enables a better identification of the personnel with the company (see Chapter 8);
7. it encourages a paternalistic attitude (see Chapter 8).

It is uncertain how long family firms will retain their place in the
construction industry for a number of reasons. First, if the firm was
founded as long as three generations ago, the shareholdings may be
in the hands of fairly distant relations and it is not necessarily in their
interests to have a large proportion of their wealth tied up in a
business with which they have tenuous, if any, links. Members of the
family may therefore be tempted to sell part or all of their shareholdings. The only way to prevent the break-up of the family firm is to
rely on trusts formed in the early stages of the firm's development.

Second, diversification into capital-intensive activities is often the
proper route for the development of a construction company. Growth
of family firms may be stunted if they are unable or unwilling to raise
funds for fear of diluting the family shareholdings. However, a
number of family firms are diversified, though perhaps not as much as
they might have been had they not been constrained from raising
funds.

Third, without sufficient family-members appropriately qualified
and willing to work in the business, the family would have difficulty in
keeping control over the management or in recruiting persons of high
calibre who would be prepared to manage within the confines of a
policy dictated by the needs of the family to retain control.

Two conglomerates, Trafalgar House and P&O, own construction
or construction-related firms which are among the thirty-five largest
firms shown on Table 1.2, as well as some smaller ones. Some of
these firms were included in the survey. The main requirement of
conglomerates from their subsidiaries is financial inasmuch as they
are expected to meet certain financial targets which may not necessarily take into account the special characteristics of contracting (see
Chapter 4).

From the construction company's point of view, ownership by a
conglomerate presents it with a number of constraints in terms of
potential growth and development. First, it may have been taken
over solely because of its positive cash flow and whereas, before

acquisition, it could decide how best to use the cash, the decision will now be made by the corporate board and too little cash may be left to the construction side (see Chapter 3). Second, if the conglomerate is diversified into housing and property (both activities which generate higher profits than contracting) the construction firm will not be able to diversify into this type of work itself and will lose opportunities to increase its profit rate (see Chapter 3).

Third, a subsidiary has to work within the capital limits which are set by the main board. 'A subsidiary cannot have its own rights issue and this impinges on the scale and timing of the company's development.'

In the interviews stress was laid on the disadvantages of being part of a conglomerate. In the companion volume in the chapter on diversification Cannon and Hillebrandt list seven advantages of a contracting firm being part of a conglomerate as follows:

1. the firm acquires greater stability through its ownership by a larger organisation and close relationships with fellow subsidiaries;
2. stability is further enhanced since the contracting company's fluctuations/cycles are different from those of the other activities of the group;
3. obtaining work may be facilitated by the reputation of the parent company, especially abroad;
4. the financial strength of the group gives the contracting subsidiary an edge over other competitors;
5. the company may have access to a wider range of fringe benefits to attract and retain skilled personnel;
6. the company may be able to exert more pressure politically;
7. the company does not have to try to maintain stable levels of performance for the benefit of the Stock Exchange.[1]

All public limited companies which are not family-controlled have to pay considerable attention to their appraisal by stockbrokers since it influences the demand for shares, including that by potential predators.

In the construction industry there have been several management buy-outs, at least one of them in the top thirty-odd companies. During the course of the project, in order to ensure completeness of approach, some discussions were held on the subject. There are a number of ways in which management buy-outs can be arranged.

One factor common to all is that they require institutional funding. The precise form of ownership arrangements varies from case to case.

7.2 THE MAIN BOARD

The degree to which the companies visited are diversified varies considerably and this is reflected in the membership of the board and in the structure of subsidiaries and functional committees.

The membership of the main board of the group ranges from eight to eighteen (norm ten to thirteen) and all but one board include a number of non-executive directors. Apart from the chief executive, the executive directors on the main board normally represent the larger separate businesses and specific functions, notably finance and occasionally personnel.

In general the management of personnel in a company is seen as a secondary level function. This is not compatible with the fact that the companies visited regarded managers as their crucial resource; that most said that they should do more training, management development and planning of management progression and that the current environment in business encourages more attention to man-management. In the majority of cases, the personnel function was not represented on the main board. Senior personnel managers felt that they did not have full backing from the board and complained that their role was sometimes limited to that of adviser to the regions where the effective decisions were taken in some companies. It may be that the type of person attracted to personnel management is not in general a decision-maker by inclination nor necessarily adequately trained in the relevant skills required for board membership. There is a vicious circle. While the personnel manager is unsuitable for board membership he will not be appointed to the board and because the personnel function is not accorded full status it is not possible to recruit first-class people to this area of business. Another reason is that operational managers look upon the personnel function as their own responsibility and rely on the personnel manager as a source of information rather than for policy-making. Even if this works well, and in some cases it undoubtedly does, it results in a piecemeal approach to personnel matters, including training and career development. This has become even more important with diversification of businesses because it is now theoretically easier to get a transfer of senior management (above site level in contracting) from contracting to other businesses and vice versa, with potential advantages to the businesses concerned.

On the whole the services department of the firm are very poorly represented on the board. This is not a disadvantage if the services in question are those where individual board members are likely to have expertise, such as surveying, but can cause complications where a subject, such as computer facilities, is not well understood.

In the great majority of companies which were visited, the membership of the company boards, whether public limited company or just limited, included a number of non-executive directors. Not surprisingly, on average those non-executive directors tended to be older than the executive members. They were likely to have worked in or still to be involved with companies whose activities were in some way connected with or relevant to those of the construction company, such as directors of building societies, or other finance institutions, or of building material producers. Some were appointed because they could play a useful political or public relations role. They were regarded as friends of the company, with an advisory role and an external view on the policy side, rather than as representatives of shareholders' interests. In some family firms there were non-executive directors in place purely because of their large shareholding. A few companies laid great stress on the full involvement of the non-executive directors in all policy decisions and on the role of the non-executive in monitoring the performance of other directors up to and including the chief executive. At the time that the interviews were conducted, there were non-executives on the boards of large construction companies which were subsidiaries of corporate organisations. In some cases of public limited companies the chairman of the company was a non-executive director.

There appears to be a conflict between the desire to ensure that the constituent parts of the company are represented on the board and the recognition that its efficient functioning requires its membership to be limited. Companies attempt to overcome this problem in several ways. One is to have an executive committee, immediately below the board, on which all operating units are represented. In one case, this committee functions almost as a main board, the latter meeting only on those occasions when formal business has to be conducted. Another is to structure the operating units in such a way that the principal activities of the company are represented on the board. This may involve one person representing a diverse group of businesses and may therefore lead to a more pyramidical structure than desired by the company. Most companies are keen to have a reasonably flat pyramid, without too many levels between first line and top management.

The division of responsibility between the chairman and the chief executive or managing director varies considerably from company to company. Where the chairman is non-executive he is involved in policy only. In some companies the division of responsibility is clear, for example, the chairman dealing with policy and the outside world and the managing director 'managing the shop'. In other companies the roles are unclear and this causes uncertainty in the lines of responsibility.

7.3   THE OPERATING UNITS

The title given to the operating parts of the companies varies as does their legal status. In some companies there is a large number of subsidiaries, varying in location, size and function. In others, the number of subsidiaries is small. In both cases, they may be referred to as operating units or be gathered together or divided into operating units. There is nothing sacrosanct about the organisation of the operating units within companies and in several companies steps had recently been taken, or were proposed, to alter the number and structure of the operating units.

The reasons put forward for changes in the structure of companies vary. They included an awareness that the current organisational structure was no longer compatible with the operations of the company; the need to change following acquisitions, mergers or indeed sales of part of the operations; decisions to diversify internally or to shift the balance of the company's business in new or different directions and to respond to advice from external consultants or experts. Indeed, on this last point, it was suggested that one reason for bringing in consultants was to obtain confirmation from them that changes proposed, but perhaps not wholly supported within the company, were those which ought to be made. One company said that in any case change was desirable after a certain time to allow restructuring and to make new promotions.

Other reasons for change in structure or organisation should be mentioned. In several companies, a number of board members and senior managers, appointed in junior posts in the early 1950s are now reaching retirement age. Many of these came to the companies with degrees in the engineering sciences. As they relinquish their full-time employment, their seats are being taken by a younger generation, with skills in a broader range of disciplines. 'A new broom sweeps clean' is as good a truism as ever and these younger men are understandably keen to exercise their newly acquired power by making some changes in the organisations which they now control.

Second, as mentioned in other chapters, the role of construction companies has changed from that of principal to that of agent, which implies the development of new areas of expertise and a reorganis-ation of some of the functions of those companies. New and broader developments in the areas of marketing, procurement and finance in particular, call for changes in the way in which some of these companies have been structured until now.

Third, the introduction of information technology into companies is usually accompanied by some organisational and structural changes. There is first of all the establishment of a new services function which has to be fitted into the overall structure of the company. It is usual to set it alongside the financial or management services, though in the early stages, it is linked to the part of the organisation where it is first used, which could be in surveying or site operations. It is because information technology tended to be intro-duced in one particular area of the company rather than planned for the company as a whole that expensive mistakes were made in the past. It could, however, be claimed with some justification that the speed of technological change has been such that the number of firms which have not made poor decisions are few and far between.

Examples of the reasons put forward by three different companies for organisational change are given below. They emphasise some of the points made above.

The monitoring of activities which until recently seemed to have been at a very low level is also increasing. The reason for the low level of central control and monitoring in the past is that when the group consisted almost entirely of construction activities, the whole and the parts were almost synonymous. When the expansion geographically and into other activities took place, with the sub-division of the group into more operating units, the control and monitoring processes were not increased *pari passu*. At the same time the changes in the environment and in group policies mean that more monitoring and control and more sophistication may be necessary.

and

One of the main objectives of the restructuring is to ensure that the various operating divisions of the building company learn from each other's experience in all areas of the business instead of operating in rather watertight compartments each with its own strengths and weaknesses. It will also unify the company so that it operates as a whole rather than as a number or separate parts.

and again, on the same theme,

There has been very little cross-fertilisation of ideas from one region of the building and civil engineering operations to another. This will be corrected with the new structure.

It will be obvious that the greater the number of operating units the greater the importance of ensuring that their management is properly and formally set up. This will be more costly and time-intensive than in companies where the main components of the company are small in number. Not only will the administration costs be larger the larger the number of subsidiaries, but other costs such as those of auditing, taxation and legal services will also be considerably greater. If one takes the example of taxation, a company with subsidiaries say, in excess of 100, has to prepare separate audited accounts and tax submissions for each and every one of its subsidiaries. There are no short cuts. At the same time, the greater the number of subsidiaries the easier it is for the company to reward its managers by giving them the status of director. This particular strategy fits in well with Williamson's five types of reward: power, prestige, salary, status and security.[2]

It can, however, lead to over-large boards. One group's important subsidiary board was judged to be too big: 'in the past board membership was a means of giving status and it seems that the board has been allowed to grow beyond the size of maximum efficiency'.

There is a very decentralised structure in all the contracting companies. All said that they allowed their operating units, however defined, to work as separate businesses with autonomy on day-to-day matters. However, the implementation of this policy varied greatly from one company to another. In some cases there are elaborate requirements from head office for various returns from site and from the regions on a daily, weekly, monthly or quarterly basis; procedures are laid down as to the way in which sites and subsidiaries and regions are to be run; numerous formal meetings take place and there are a number of committees; a large input is made from service departments at head office and there are strict limits of authority on the permitted capital expenditure, contract size and type to be undertaken, and managerial staffing. At the other extreme there are requirements for referring to head office decisions only on capital expenditure above certain levels and senior staff appointments. There is always a requirement for financial reporting at regular intervals. However these arrangements operate only as long as the performance of the operating unit comes up to the expectations of the divisional or main board. If performance is not satisfactory the contact between senior head office managers and site managers increases rapidly, more information has to be given to head office and ultimately changes in site management might be effected.

An example of the way that the arrangements work in practice is given by one company where it was said that:

One of the features of the management structure of the group is the very substantial autonomy of its parts with generally 100 per cent of control by the operating unit of the projects it undertakes, though with some control from head office over capital expenditure and staff. Generally if the unit makes a good profit and has a satisfactory return on capital employed, it is allowed to run its own business.

Nevertheless the attention given by the director in charge to each part of the business under his control varies enormously. He goes to *all* the board meetings of one company but rarely to others. 'He needs to be satisfied that the operating unit is progressing on the right lines and that, for example, it is not taking an over-optimistic view of the market.'

It is quite possible to be decentralised but with strong control. One senior executive who said that overall the group was very decentralised, then went on to say that there was a meeting on each Monday morning of the available members of the board where good and bad news was reported. The managing director would after that be in close touch with operating units to discuss problems which had been reported and to satisfy himself that all necessary steps were taken. It was pointed out that this was in line with the view that the board should only coordinate, otherwise ensuring that there was good management at a lower level and allowing that management the responsibility to act.

The degree of autonomy given to an operating unit affects the extent to which it has its own services specific to that unit or whether it uses pooled centrally provided services. A few companies have strong central services departments, for example, estimating, surveying, personnel, purchasing, and some design. In some companies this is a matter of philosophy but in others it is seen as a straight matter of efficiency:

> The subsidiary companies, because of their relatively small size, cannot afford their own specialist resources and they rely on advisory services which are freely available to them and which are centralised. There is scope for those advisory services to play a more critical role . . .

or

> With so many units within the group it may be wasteful for each to provide its own services where there is a common component for the division or group as a whole.

In other companies however the services functions are located mainly in the regional or functional parts of the organisation with sometimes a small back-up organisation in the head office. Each system has its merits.

Strong head-office services enable a uniformity in the approach of the group in the various service areas and facilitate the better use of staff since the situation of one part of the organisation being short of, say, estimators and another having a surplus does not arise. While services are established mainly in the operating units, there is a more integrated regional or functional team and the greater contact between the services personnel and other operations in the company facilitates promotion across boundaries of professions or skills. If there is a work overload in one part of the organisation specialists are sometimes borrowed from another part which is temporarily underused.

An interesting organisational problem often arises with plant. Some years ago one company had changed the operation of the plant company in the group. At one time the plant company operated only for the group contracts and plant was hired at 10 per cent below the market rate. Profit was made on the contract itself. However as a *quid pro quo* contracting companies in the group were required to use the in-house plant company. If the plant company did not have the equipment required it would hire it and rehire it to the contracting company. This became very inefficient because the plant company had no measure of efficiency and no control over its investment decisions. Now the plant company hires out at competitive market rates. The contracting companies may go to other plant hire companies and the in-house plant hire company may do business with other contractors. The plant company makes a profit and is efficient and competitive.

In the opinion of the interviewers, the one function where it is very important to have both a central and an operating location is personnel. The central location is essential because transfers from one part of the organisation to another need to be made as part of the training operation and to obtain the best fit of jobs and people. A strong policy of training, and monitoring of development of managers should be centrally developed. This need for a stronger personnel function has also been mentioned in comments on the composition of the main board in Section 7.1 above.

There are differences in the extent to which firms integrate recently acquired companies into the organisation of the group. Even in cases where the new companies are in the same business as the purchasing company the latter may retain the name and identity of the newly acquired ones, allowing them to continue as heretofore, subject only to careful monitoring. On the other hand a company may have been acquired with the sole objective of acquiring scarce management resources or of retaining only a part of it and integrating that part within the group as a whole. This may not always be an easy or successful process. One of the companies interviewed had merged many years earlier with a company in a related but different field and had imposed its management on the new acquisition. The result was that the staff left and the recently acquired side of the business died.

7.4 DECISION-MAKING

There is considerable diversity in the way in which decisions are taken. Some companies have formalised systems with, for example, subcommittees of the board, or committees set up by the board either to report to it or with delegated authority. Below main board level there may be similar formal structures. Other companies were proud that they did not set up committees but in these cases informal meetings were important as the means of hammering out a course of action. In all companies a number of decisions are taken over the telephone especially where a speedy reaction to a problem is needed.

The theory of groups should be helpful in assessing the purposes of committees and less formal meetings and some aspects of this theory are discussed in the companion volume by Male and Stocks.[3] They conclude that:

> Formal meetings should, therefore, be encouraged, adhered to, and executive team members should participate in the decision making process. Leadership style becomes a further consideration in this respect. Group norms influence an individual's perceptions and the strength of a norm's influence depends positively on the group being highly cohesive. The norm should be highly relevant and each member should understand the group criteria.
>
> When dealing with complex problems, it has been shown that loosely structured groups have an initial advantage. However, tightly structured groups learn to communicate faster as they progress through the problem and their performance eventually becomes just as good as loosely structured groups.[4] Interpersonal conflict is always present to some extent in groups where members have different values, attitudes, beliefs and behaviour. A group develops its own unique culture and character as it becomes formalised and structured (Male and Stocks, p. 103, reference number altered).

In the past three or four years two or three companies have asked management consultants to examine the organisation of the whole group with the result that a number of changes have been introduced. These were firms which had not updated their method of working at group level to keep up with the changed nature of their business and with its increased diversity.

In the remainder of the companies several are sceptical about the ability of management consultants to improve the broad operation of the company, partly because investigations by management consultants had not always been satisfactory. Specific consultancies for more technical matters were more favourably regarded.

7.5 FORMAL AND INFORMAL COMMUNICATIONS SYSTEMS

There is a similar diversity in the channels for information flow. Some information is communicated at meetings and the existence of formal committees probably ensures some more general dispersal of information. Complete informality of communication occurs only when the channels have been in operation a long time between people well-known to each other. The hub of the management communication system on construction in one company is mainly by personal contact on the telephone or face to face with the managing director, who is given or asks for information, is the source of advice to all parts of the organisation and takes decisions as necessary. This system is very dependent on the personality of the man concerned and the respect and affection felt for him. Another more formal system would be necessary at his retirement.

One company partly blamed what it called the 'agent syndrome' for poor flows of information. This is the attitude of the site agent who wishes to manage his own site undisturbed by others. This attitude, it was said, could extend outside the site to other parts of the organisation.

Information is not only necessary to enable decisions to be taken. It is also necessary as part of good staff relations. Some companies try hard to tell the senior managers what is happening across the whole company by meetings, by get-togethers over a weekend, by using particular occasions to widen the knowledge of senior managers.

In contrast, another company had no formal communication procedure. 'The company does not communicate much to employees about success or otherwise. This is related to the philosophy of the organisation.'

It is relatively rare for any group of people to query the efficiency of the communications network with which they operate. It has usually evolved over a period of time, adjusts at the margin as people move between functions and roles, and is largely taken for granted. Because there are no rules to regulate the way in which the informal system works, it is less likely to be formally analysed and reviewed. This is of course not so for the formal system which can be altered and restructured.

Both systems operate side by side, if not on top of each other, in all companies so that it is quite difficult to analyse and assess how well they perform either individually or together, and it would be very difficult to categorise them. However, certain general statements can be made. In those companies where the size of the head office is very deliberately kept small, the favoured communications system is informal and is demonstrably informal within the head office and more formal – though still kept simple – between head office and the operating units.

Where the head office is a large organisation the formal system dominates and in at least one case involves a complicated network of committees and meetings which leads to the suspicion that it is, to a degree, ossifying. The internal organisation seems least formal within the international subsidiaries, because distance requires a different, more flexible approach which automatically leads to a more informal communication network, though they are probably at their most formal in their relationships with foreign clients. Communications from the board to the employees take the form of an in-house magazine where the focus, as would be expected, is on company achievements in the industry and personal ones in the company. They deal almost exclusively with past events.

7.6　RELATIONSHIP BETWEEN THEORY AND PRACTICE

There are three chapters in the companion volume which are partially or wholly relevant to the organisation and structure of firms. First, the chapter on manpower management (Section 8.2.2) by Buckley and Enderwick discusses hierarchical employment relationships.[5] The authors outline Williamson's model which 'focuses on tasks which are non-homogeneous' and 'involve high costs of management time as transactions are negotiated and executed' (p. 111). A solution to some of these problems is provided by a hierarchical structure, of which the two basic forms identified by Williamson are the unitary structure (U Form) and the multidivisional one (M Form).[6]

Second, the work by Male and Stocks on managers and the organisation refers to several typologies of hierarchical structures and they relate these to the construction firm.[7] They say that the typology of Miles and Snow:[8]

identifies four strategic company management types: defender, prospector, analyser and reactor. The defender company aims at stability and efficiency. It will tend to favour a formal hierarchical structure with extensive division of labour and strong central control. Information systems will be complex and vertical. Coordination mechanisms are likely to be simple and conflict will be resolved through hierarchical channels.

The prospector company will lay great stress on achieving flexibility by means of an informal and decentralised organisation with low division of labour. Information flows will tend to be horizontal and simple but there are likely to be complex mechanisms for coordination.

The analyser company comes somewhere in between the first two, aiming at the same time at stability and flexibility. The structure of an organisation will be loose with moderate central control. The coordination mechanisms will tend to be extremely complex and expensive. Conflicts will be resolved in many ways including hierarchical channels.

Lastly there is the reactor company which is unable to adopt a clear structure and will often show characteristics of the three previous types. Hence it is unstable. The organisation lacks a consistent set of response patterns to a changing environment (Male and Stocks, pp. 99–100).

None of these typologies seems to apply particularly to large construction companies. The extensive division of labour, which is related to stability, does not occur in construction as perhaps in some manufacturing industry. Construction companies are more of the prospector or analyser type though the complex and expensive coordination mechanisms occur in only one or two of the construction companies visited. There was a small number of companies which did not appear to be sufficiently well organised and could be regarded as reactor companies.

A second way of classifying structures is more hierarchical and discussed as follows:

Parsons[9] suggests there are three levels in the structure of any firm: the technical or production level, the organisational or managerial level and the institutional or community level. Kast and Rosenzweig[10] have adapted these into three hierarchical levels, interdependent systems that are present in any medium to large sized company. These systems are referred to as the technical system, the organisational level and the institutional level. The first, the technical system, is involved with the actual task performance of the organisation. For a contracting company this would be the site. Secondly, there is the organisational level which coordinates and integrates the task performance of the technical system and the institutional system. At this level the primary function of management is the integration of people, information and material inputs to the technical and institutional levels. In the contracting company the buying, estimating and planning departments would be examples within the organisational level. The contracts manager would be an example of an integrator at the organisational level. Thirdly, the institutional level is concerned with relating and adapting the activities of the company to the business environment within which it operates. Kast and Rosenzweig argue that these three interdependent levels form the managerial system, span the entire organisation and integrate technology, people, resources and the company with the environment. However, since each level deals with different inputs, outputs and levels of uncertainty, managers will require a different orientation and sets of skills in order to deal with the requirements of their job (Male and Stocks, p. 100, reference numbers altered).

These levels are similar to those described in the third chapter in the companion volume relevant to this subject – that by Clark on the social technology approach. He distinguishes four main levels in the firm:[11]

Another approach is to think of the whole structure as a series of substructures or layers from the direct operating units through site and project management and the technostructure, the top layer taking decisions such as choice of market and financial objectives. Each of these layers would comprise a number of work units and the higher up in the firm the more the work units are involved with long-term issues rather than the present time frame. The theoretical assumption is that any of the work units in each layer may and should possess different structures yet all are integrated in the total structure[12] (Clark, pp. 78–80, reference number altered).

The social technology approach described by Clark suggests that the organisation of the processes in the firm and the firm's structure should be related both to the degree to which the information inputs to the process are stable and uniform and to the extent to which they are understood. Clark's thesis is that in the twenty years to 1986 the inputs to the construction process have become more stable, more uniform and better understood. He gives examples of material inputs:

> There have been moves towards standardisation in the construction industry, particularly in the 1960s which saw the beginning of system building, and the prefabrication of components, the establishment of the *agrément* system and the creation of design packages. Many in the industry would argue that this trend has recently been reversed with more difficult sites leading to one-off buildings, even greater choice in materials and components and ever increasing variety in contractual arrangements. The important factor for the theory of social technology is not only – or even mainly – the variety and complexity of the inputs to construction, but the ability to order the information available so that the inputs to the decision making process can be more standardised. Thus there may now be more information available in a better ordered manner about a greater variety of materials and components than previously when there were few materials and components but with too little information about them. In spite of the proliferation of materials and components, the decision maker may perceive his choice as being a simpler one now than hitherto, especially with the assistance of computer-aided design (CAD) and computer-aided management (CAM) (Clark, p. 86).

This would result in 'an increasing certainty in the inputs to top decision making' (Clark, p. 86). In this case, according to the theory the whole structure of the firm should move towards routine procedures with few exceptions.

The interviewees with whom these matters were discussed did not see any great move towards better understood, more stable information in contracting firms. Part of the difference between Clark and the interviewees seems to be due to the fact that Clark includes in his model parts of the process which have little to do with contracting organisations and are in general in the purview of the design team in the traditional process. Thus choice of materials and computer-aided design are not contracting matters in the traditional sense, though they do become so in design-and-build contracts. However, Clark lays considerable emphasis on the traditional tendering process.

In this traditional process it seems unlikely that the quality and stability of information on some inputs have improved. The reason is that the rapid changes in the methods of employing labour and the recent substantial rise in rates for labour-only subcontracting, which respond to the fluctuations of the market, lead to less good information and less stable data. In the 1960s the overall market for construction was on an upward trend, broken by pauses. In the 1970s and the 1980s there have been dramatic changes in workload which have unsettled the labour market, the price of plant and the supply of and demand for management. It is unlikely that improvements in information in other matters have been sufficient to offset these uncertainties.

The next matter to consider is the level of the construction firm which is being analysed. Even if the information inputs at the level of the tender were more stable, the construction firm trying to differentiate its construction product (see Chapter 2) and increasingly diversified (see Chapter 3) is not necessarily facing any diminution in uncertain, unstable, not-well-understood factors in other areas of the business.

In his outline of the social technology framework, Clark anticipates a movement from a decentralised system with a technostructure with low discretion and power but site management with high discretion and power, to a centralised system though still with some flexibility where the discretion and power of the technostructure is high and that of the site management low (Clark, Figure 6.5). At the same time, he says, there would be a change in the way in which coordination within groups takes place, with the more powerful layer in the organisation operating with continual mutual adjustment and feedback, and the less powerful with more preplanning.

There is no confirmation of this change in the structure of firms. Firms do examine their structure from time to time, especially when prompted by major diversification or the need for a more efficient grouping of operations. In the majority of cases, however, this has not made the organisation more or less decentralised but has only extended or rearranged the existing system. Control by the head office over the operating units, but not normally directly over sites, has increased in many cases and there have certainly been more formal procedures for considering strategy, including planning, but these concern the levels above the site management. There was no indication in discussion with regional office managers that there had been a great change in their control over sites though this was not one of the main objectives of the project so that the question was perhaps not well tested.

It is interesting to note that, perhaps by force of circumstances rather than choice, the overseas units where information tends to be poor are more decentralised than head office operations in all companies visited.

Clark says 'If in fact the inputs to firms are becoming increasingly more ordered, and hence can be routinised, then consequent alterations should have been occurring in the structure' (Clark, p. 88). This statement is not doubted and is indeed very important. What is doubted is that the inputs *are* becoming more routinised. Furthermore the changes in the structure have not followed the pattern which would have been anticipated.

Clark goes on to say that: 'Given the competitive nature of the construction sector in the 1980s, it may be expected that those firms with inefficient structures were less profitable than others' (Clark, p. 88).

Not all firms have been equally profitable. The only evidence as to the reason for this in terms of structure is that in the less successful firms strategic planning was inadequate and there was less control though not necessarily a less, or more formal, decentralised organisation.

On the other side firms which have been reasonably successful – and it is very difficult to isolate contracting or even construction from other areas of the business – have a great diversity of organisational structure: from very decentralised to centralised, from light to tight control and from defined procedures to free choice of procedures.

7.7 EXTERNAL RELATIONSHIPS

The relations between the companies and their external environment were given time and care by all the companies studied. Because of their size and place in the industry, the fact that the Department of the Environment is their sponsor department and that the public sector has been and remains (though to a much lesser extent) an important client and certainly an important influence, they have been able to find the door of ministerial or senior civil servant offices, if not open, at least not too difficult to get through. Over the years, their contacts with members of government have operated at both the formal and informal level. The Building and Civil Engineering Economic Development Committees (EDCs) now replaced by a single body – the Construction Industry Sector Group – gave a number of senior board members the opportunity to air their views with ministers and their representatives and senior trade union members. The Group of Eight, now defunct, gave the broader industry a voice, though it was not necessarily that of a large firm. Overall, they appeared reasonably satisfied with the public relations network developed at the political level.

All the large firms undertake both building and civil engineering work and thus are members of BEC (Building Employers Confederation) and of the FCEC (Federation of Civil Engineering Contractors) where they can influence the content and direction of policy. Within BEC they belong to the National Contractors Group. At the trade association level one expects to find the names of senior members of companies in posts of responsibility at one time or another. They will be nominated to sit on committees or boards with close construction interests, such as the CIOB, or the CITB, and on academic boards. A number of them are affiliated to the CBI or members of the Institute of Directors. A few companies referred to their disenchantment with the work of trade associations. They acknowledge that one of the problems is that the best people cannot be spared to participate in federations' activities and that they are not functioning as well as they used to do. One or two companies have withdrawn from active involvement though they remain members. Outside the formal world of politics and trade associations, eleven of them who know each other well have recently formed a company to undertake inner city redevelopment.

All companies acknowledge the importance which they attach to maintaining good relations with their brokers, who were regularly invited to meet senior members of the board. They would become more closely involved with the company's affairs if a merger or takeover was in the offing. In addition the companies take care to brief stockbrokers' analysts from time to time (see also Chapter 4).

NOTES AND REFERENCES

1. Cannon, J. and Hillebrandt, P.M., 'Diversification' in Hillebrandt, P.M. and Cannon, J. (eds) *The Management of Construction Firms: Aspects of Theory* (London: Macmillan, 1989) ch. 3, p. 40.
2. Williamson, O.E., *Markets and Hierarchies: Analysis and Anti-trust Implications – A Study in the Economics of Internal Organisation* (New York: Free Press and Collier Macmillan, 1975).
3. Male, S. and Stocks, R., 'Managers and the Organisation' in Hille-

brandt, P.M. and Cannon, J. (eds) *The Management of Construction Firms: Aspects of Theory* (London: Macmillan, 1989) ch. 7. This source is often quoted and is indicated simply by Male and Stocks and page or section numbers.

4. Mintzberg, H., *The Structuring of Organisations* (Englewood Cliffs, New Jersey: Prentice Hall, 1979) p. 106.
5. Buckley, P.J. and Enderwick, P., 'Manpower Management' in Hillebrandt, P.M. and Cannon, J. (eds) *The Management of Construction Firms: Aspects of Theory* (London: Macmillan, 1989) ch. 8.
6. These are mentioned in Cannon, J. and Hillebrandt, P.M., 'Theories of the Firm' in Hillebrandt, P.M. and Cannon, J. (eds) *The Management of Construction Firms: Aspects of Theory* (London: Macmillan, 1989) ch. 1.
7. See note 2.
8. Miles, R.E., Snow, C.C., Meyer, A.D. and Coleman, H.J. Jr, 'Organisational Strategy, Structure and Process', *Academy of Management Review* (July 1978) pp. 552, 554 and 556.
9. Parsons, T. *Structure and Process in Modern Societies* (New York: The Free Press of Glencoe, 1960) pp. 60–96.
10. Kast, F.E. and Rosenzweig, J.E., 'The Modern View: a Systems Approach' in *Systems Behaviour*, 3rd edn, Open Systems Group (London: Harper & Row, 1981) pp. 52–6.
11. Clark, P. 'Social Technology and Structure' in Hillebrandt, P.M. and Cannon, J. (eds) *The Management of Construction Firms: Aspects of Theory* (London: Macmillan, 1989) ch. 6. This source is often quoted and is indicated simply by Clark and page or section numbers.
12. The differentiation between work units in the same firm and the problems of integration are addressed very fully in Lawrence, P.R. and Lorsch, J., *Organisation and Environment: Matching Differentiation and Integration* (Cambridge, Mass: Harvard University Press, 1967).

Part IV
Human Resources

8 The Management Resource

8.1 THE IMPORTANCE OF MANAGEMENT

It is the quantity and quality of management which determines whether a contracting firm is efficient or inefficient. In contracting firms the main scarce resource is management. Of the other resources capital assets are small, materials are important but outside the direct control of the contractor, labour may be scarce but if so it is scarce for all contractors in a particular area.

Management in contracting is particularly important because of some of the characteristics of the industry:

1. each project has to be set up as a production unit on a fresh site starting from nothing;
2. the fact that the industry is very labour-intensive means that good man-management is vital to the success of a project;
3. the production process is very complex involving a large number of inputs;
4. it is uncertain, because of the weather and ground conditions as well as of the practical difficulty of guaranteeing that all supplies of materials, equipment and labour will be there on time. Thus, the number of management decisions to be taken is large and the industry at site level is very decision-intensive;
5. at the level of the operating unit, each project is different and has different clients and professionals, so management relations with outside organisations may be complex.
6. because of the wide geographical dispersion of activities it is often difficult for the site manager and sometimes for the operating unit manager to obtain help or decisions from head office. This is especially so in overseas work where the managers have to be capable of operating and taking decisions without the benefit of prior consultation.

There is another aspect of the industry which has an important bearing on the management resource and that is the dominance of the specialist professional. Whereas in other industries, generalists

115

are more likely to fill senior management posts, in construction, senior posts are filled by heads of the production divisions (building, civil engineering, homes and plant) who have been trained in surveying, civil engineering and related sciences.

This chapter concentrates on construction managers as they are the resource which can be obtained only within the industry, unlike managers in finance, personnel or other service functions within the firm who are transferable across industries. Chapter 6 deals with the special requirements for overseas work.

8.2   MANAGEMENT PLANNING

The importance of management in the construction industry means that it is vital to have the right type of managers in place at all times. The success or failure of each project hinges on the management team on site. Management planning is therefore an important aspect of company policy. One very senior executive, brandishing a set of monthly financial data, project-based and aggregated, observed that all companies tended to focus too much on financial resources and paid too little heed to human resources data: 'I want to see human resources data alongside the financial data in order to plan the company's future.' One company has a three-year plan which focuses on finance, business and people. The last element includes the identification of gaps for promotion and training needs.

In construction, each project is short term and each new site requires its own management team. Management planning is therefore concerned with the transfer of management to form new teams, with training and promotion to foster new management resources and with recruitment of managers from outside the company. The last includes both recruitment from subsidiaries within a group and recruitment from other companies. The decision to bid for any project therefore implies a number of tasks to be carried out and absorbed by existing departments in head office (surveying, purchasing, recruitment, etc.) and setting up a new management team. That is where the potential for internal growth and success lies.

Management planning in construction should have a more important role than in many other industries where growth of output may be met simply by, for example, increasing overtime without any changes or additions to the managerial strength or structure of the firm.

It may be because the efficiency of individual sites depends partly on good working relations within short-lived management teams that the company culture was given more importance in interviews than might have been expected. Culture may be described as the attitudes of the existing management with respect not only to the way that the business is run and its relations with the outside world but also the managers' own lifestyle. Where the formation of new teams is an important part of management planning, the process is eased if managers clearly understand and support the company culture.

Management planning in large construction firms should also consider the size and the age-structure of its managerial force and earmark high flyers from whom will be selected the future members of its senior hierarchy. This function is more developed in some companies than in others.

As one company puts it:

> Succession planning is undertaken by each division and then at group level. Planning of management development is however not yet undertaken satisfactorily. It has been agreed in principle that a management development plan is desirable but in practice little progress has been made.

But in another company:

> 'The group undertakes an annual appraisal of the management personnel situation and an assessment is made of the potential of each person in senior management. The problem of succession is considered.'

All companies were aware that there were two stages in the promotion process where specific steps had to be taken to prepare managers for selection to higher posts. The first stage is that of transfer from site management to regional office or head office. The second is that of promotion to membership of policy-making groups. At least one senior executive believed that the move from site management to contracts manager was the harder one in terms of ensuring that the contracts manager refrained from interfering on his old home ground.

The first stage requires acceptance by the manager of a wider range of responsibilities as well as a change in roles which includes loss of direct physical control over the construction process and loss of identity with projects which he regarded as his own in terms of wider relationships within the regional company. Some formal training at head office is usually offered by the company at this stage (see Section 8.5.6).

The second stage, the move to more generalist functions, is met by different measures in the companies which were visited, though in most cases they use a combination of formal internal and external training with opportunities for role-playing.

In those companies where the preparation and discussion of the five-year plan is formalised, more attention is paid to the issue of succession than in those companies where the furthest horizon is three years hence (the current year plus two).

It would appear therefore that in major construction companies the personnel function should have a larger role than in other industries, both in terms of the analysis which it should carry out as a matter of routine into the age and profile structure of the company's management and in terms of training and its role of allocating the scarce management to operating units and sites. It is suggested in Chapter 7 that this function is not always given the importance it requires.

8.3 MOTIVATION OF MANAGERS

Growth has desirable and welcome rewards for managers in terms of increased status, responsibility and power, as well as financial rewards and security.

In the companion volume Male and Stocks stated:[1]

> The needs for power, affiliation and achievement are among the most important in understanding organisational behaviour.
> The need for power has been found to be the best predictor of managerial success and it is therefore often regarded as the most important for those whose goal is to become managers or supervisors.[2] Indeed power and also conflict are seen as central features of organisational life. The need for affiliation is related to the desire to form interpersonal relationships. It is a particularly important motivational drive in group dynamics. Hunt[3] argues that 60 per cent of the workforce are more concerned with forming and maintaining relationships rather than expressing the needs for power or achievement. Whereas the needs for power and achievement are more important at executive level, the fulfilment of

affiliative or relationship needs therefore tends to dominate the thinking of people at the bottom of the organisational hierarchy. In the construction industry context affiliative needs may be particularly important at site operative level. The need for achievement has been found to be characteristic of entrepreneurs[4] (pp. 93–4).

No real assessment of the motivation of site managers was possible, since this was not part of the research project. However, the nature of the job suggests that site managers rate achievement and power highly and in general appreciate the need for affiliation to the site team.

Promotion above the level of the site management involves less direct control over operations and this may be one of the reasons why the site manager often experiences problems in adapting to being a contracts managers or moving to more business-oriented functions.

Financial rewards are clearly an important aspect of motivation. Rewards for construction industry managers are discussed in Section 8.5.5 below. They are low compared with many other industries.

The general view was that motivation is maintained or enhanced by paying special attention to job satisfaction – 'concrete job satisfaction'. Salary, security and satisfaction were quoted as what people sought in a job. 'Motivation stems from the job satisfaction of seeing what people produce, it is there because they don't do the same thing twice, because it isn't a 9-to-5 job.'

Motivation is generated and maintained because there is always change taking place in the company which makes acquisitions, sells companies, creates companies and moves people across where there are gaps or new jobs to be filled. In this way, people are kept content and their performance is also enhanced because the small size of the subsidiary companies encourages good informal communications and a friendly environment.

The importance of the friendly set-up was mentioned with reference to other construction companies where the organisation was much more formal and the chairman hardly ever seen, even by quite senior employees.

It is interesting that a good communication system is seen in some companies as a means of maintaining morale and motivation: 'One way of generating or maintaining motivation is through involving people heavily in "team briefings". People work better if they know what is going on.' It was emphasised that construction changes all the time: new teams are put together, new projects are won, new clients are gained, so part of the excitement and motivation lies in the fact of continuous change. The good site manager is one who knows how to motivate people below him.

In one company 'the method of communicating with the staff at large is partly a house magazine' but the opinion was expressed by a senior member of the management team that he would like to know more of what was happening in the group as a whole, though he did not *need* to know it to carry out his job efficiently'.

There had certainly been recent improvements in a number of companies, for example, in one company all senior managers meet once a year either at a group conference or a dinner. At the conference each managing director explains what his unit is doing.

8.4   MANAGERIAL ROLES

It is stressed by Male and Stocks that is is important to have roles clearly defined and well balanced:

> Role ambiguity results when there is some uncertainty in the mind either of the individual or of the membership of his role set, as to precisely what his role is at any given time.[5] Role overload occurs where the number of different roles which one person holds becomes too much for him. This is not the same as work overload. Role underload, on the other hand, results in a person believing he can cope with either a larger role or a greater number of roles than he presently fills.
>
> Role stress takes two forms, either role pressure or role strain. The former is seen by Handy[6] to be beneficial stress whilst the latter is harmful stress. People need some stress to bring out the best in them although too much can be harmful. A difficulty for the manager is knowing how much stress an individual can handle and this is particularly relevant in construction especially at project level where it is difficult to gauge the site manager's ability to cope with larger or more complex situations (p. 95, reference numbers altered).

The problem of balance of load and roles arises at all levels including the board as described by a contractor:

One of the problems is the need for senior managers, up to and including the main board, to balance the need to be involved with the day-to-day decision-making in order to have a thorough grasp and control over the business with the need to have time to devote to the long-term strategy and innovation. Prior to the organisation of board responsibilities and the chief executive divesting himself of any line-management responsibility the board had almost certainly too much day-to-day involvement. The impression is still that there is much time spent on short-term matters in the main board but the balance is improved. It is important that the boards of subsidiary companies also seek the correct balance.

The balance between various functions on site and the delineation of roles is important, as is evidenced by the need to remind works managers that it is the site agent who is in charge (see Section 8.5.1 below).

Several classifications of roles have been produced. Some of these are discussed in the companion volume. Classifications of roles have practical value in providing a logical framework or checklist with which to assess the performance of managers.

8.5 RECRUITMENT, PROMOTION AND TRAINING

8.5.1 Characteristics of construction managers

Many of the specific attributes of a good construction manager mentioned by contractors are typical of those you would expect to meet in all industries. Those mentioned include: technical and organisational abilities; the ability to assess alternative solutions to a problem and to take decisions in a consistent manner; the ability to distinguish between large and small issues; toughness tempered by compassion; loyalty to the company, business integrity and a moral standard; above-average intelligence, the ability to cope under stress and a will to win.

The crucial role of managers in all firms is obvious but in those industries which are labour-intensive, the management function is especially concerned with the organisation and use of human resources. Hence, the quality of management, judged in terms of man-management, is the relevant criterion. This is particularly true of the construction industry where physical separation between sites and head offices and the unique conditions prevailing on each site add to the management function a dimension not encountered in other industries.

There are however some attributes which were placed very high on the list of those required of a good manager at site level. There were three main ones:

1. *Ability to manage, control and motivate men* is vital for a construction site manager. There are a considerable number of men of diverse skills working on site for only short periods within different teams. In a very short space of time the site manager has to be able to assert his authority, motivate each group to perform well and iron out any disagreements between or within groups. Simultaneously he has to ensure that the whole site process is working well, with men, materials and plant appropriately placed and on time. He also has to deal with the design team, suppliers of materials and plant who are all external to the site itself.

2. *Ability to make quick assessments and to intervene when necessary.* There are a number of diverse operations grouped on site at any one time. The picture is constantly changing. Though there will be a site plan in greater or lesser detail, there is no visual plan of what each part of the operation should look like at any one time. This contrasts sharply with manufacturing plant where the pattern is repeated each day and perhaps every few minutes. The site manager has therefore to be able to take in and assess very quickly whether and where intervention is necessary.

3. *Independence.* Because each site is different and geographically separate from regional or head office, the site manager must be able to manage without recourse to constant consultations or meetings with his supervisors or advisers. He has to be able to make the right decisions quickly and on his own responsibility.

Companies differed in the stress they laid on these attributes and perhaps the emphasis placed expressed to some extent the different cultures of the companies to which so many referred. Independence is particularly important when companies have substantial operations abroad because there is no available back-up at close range (see Chapter 6).

An interesting example of the importance attached by one of the companies interviewed to man-management is their system by which the site agent in charge of the site works with a works manager who is responsible for the management of the men on site and also for plant. His work and functions leave the site agent free to deal with the contractual side of the project. The works managers are responsible to the site agents yet are so influential that it was necessary for this responsibility to be restated only a few years ago, and this must be so because the site agent is the person named in the contract as responsible for all site operations. The system of using works managers with its focus on man-management is applied both to building and civil engineering contracts and the success of the company in the latter is attributed partly to this method of operation.

However, some types of contracting activity require a different kind of manager. In particular management contracting was referred to by many of those interviewed as calling for a different type of person. As one contractor put it, 'the manager in management contracting has less to do with the men on site and more to do with fellow-contractors and professionals. It is more of a team effort in management contracting and not so much "them and us".'

8.5.2 Internal promotion versus external appointment

In any situation the company must assess its needs for staff and relate them to those whom it can promote from inside and those it must recruit from outside. To some extent the ratio is determined by the success of the company in planning its management progression (see Section 8.2 above). All companies without exception preferred to meet their needs for personnel from internal development and promotion because this helped to develop mutual understanding and trust.

One senior executive explained that:

Most persons at senior management level have been in the company a long time and many were recruited as trainees . . . It was pointed out that on many occasions when an outsider had been appointed, the arrangement had not worked and the appointee had not remained long in the company . . .

In another company:

'The group policy is to grow most of our own management. About a third of the managers at the top of the organisation come to the group as trainees or soon afterwards.'

In yet another company:

> It might be difficult for an outsider to survive in the company
> because it is not very participative and its band of skills is relatively
> narrow. The company now recognises the need for line managers
> to come from a wider professional range.

In at least two companies several members of the board were all
together in the 1940s. (Note that there will be problems when they all
retire together.)

The policy of internal promotion as the general rule tended to be
more prevalent in family firms:

> 'The whole ethos of the employment of personnel throughout the
> business is one of permanence. The group is paternalistic in its
> approach and very rarely dismisses staff.'

However, there were exceptions to the policy of internal promotion in all companies including family ones. Indeed several
companies now had a policy of recruiting up to one-third from
outside. The main reasons for external recruitment were as follows:

1. the growth of the group;
2. the greater degree of specialisation in the industry and higher
   technical component;
3. the growth of different forms of contracting, notably management
   contracting which needed rather different types of skills;
4. the need for people who had different ideas as a means of
   encouraging innovative thought and the development of better
   practice;
5. the wish to test the market in order to ensure that conditions of
   employment and remuneration within the company were competitive;
6. the remedy for deficiencies in management development in the
   past;
7. problems caused by unforeseen increases in work.

8.5.3 Internal promotion

Internal promotion in the construction hierarchy may be promotion
from assistant site manager to site manager and then to managing a

larger site. The particular characteristics of the person required in these jobs will be similar and include the three specific to construction mentioned in Section 8.5.1 above. The next stage is from site manager to regional office function or contracts manager where the three specific construction abilities become less important. Promotion, however, does require the exercise of new skills though not all companies considered that this led to major problems. The contracts manager may experience difficulty in determining how much he should advise or direct the action of the site agent. A good contracts manager should often allow the site agent to manage the project as he sees fit, and should not impose his own style of management. Other main stream construction managers at regional level begin to need the same skills as those required at head office policy formulation level, that is, for example, more understanding of financial matters, of marketing and of the broader aspects of running a business. Some of these skills can be learned – particularly those of finance and to some extent marketing, but others need to be developed by experience. In some companies there is an effort to bring people in from site to the regions and give them marketing and estimating experience before promotion to branch manager. Nevertheless there was a generally felt need for some training provision to help staff to make these transitions.

One company summarised its views as follows:

(a) There is difficulty in the transfer from a site agent to a visiting agent. He now has to assess and judge efficiency and performance from visits only and the problem arises of when to suggest, to tell or to do oneself – in other words the problem of delegation.

(b) The site agent will have been dealing with clients, professionals, suppliers, as well as with production matters so it is not a completely new world when he moves to the regional office.

(c) The district or visiting manager or specialist within the regional office will have had experience of regional problems before promotion to regional director and similarly on the civil engineering site.

In spite of various means of facilitating the transfer, the problem remains of how to develop a business manager from essentially a production manager. Handling of financial data is a problem. The company has looked at and tried courses at Henley, Manchester

Business School, London Business School and INSEAD (European Institute of Business Administration). Top management workshops in France were cancelled because of lack of support. Generally, the best way is exposure to the job, but they do try to run their own internal training as well. Persons commenting on the in-house training thought that it was generally good, but pointed out that basically they were training people in the ways they had used in the past rather than those suitable for the future.

Other companies reported similarly on their problems in transfer and training of senior managers though with a gradation of satisfaction or otherwise with the results. One company reported that:

It is now becoming more usual to move personnel from one (construction) company to another, particularly between one region and another. [With a few exceptions] the conditions of employment are common throughout the company and . . . it makes transfer easy . . . Transfer takes place fairly often under a salary of £20 000 but not above this level.

However, another said more or less the opposite:

It is getting much more difficult to move personnel geographically, for example, from Scotland to England, and the policy has become much more to have tight teams of people in locations where they are contented. People now look for more regional security whereas at one time they were mobile.

One of the problems in moving personnel geographically is the high cost of housing. Transfers between building and civil engineering, or rather, one way – from civil engineering to building – were favourably regarded.

The lack of distinction in organisational terms between building and civil engineering means that managers can be switched. However, this is a one-way flow. Civil engineers are put onto the management of building projects but builders are not put onto the management of civil engineering work because they do not have the right technical knowledge.

In another company which had a split between building and civil engineering, a senior staff member regretted the split because it made it more difficult to move managers around and make the best use of those available.

There was, however, relatively little attempt or support for transfers between companies in different businesses within the group to broaden views and attitudes. Indeed a number of comments were made on the different types of skills required to ensure the success of a firm's range of activities. A contractor was not considered to be suitable management material for the development side of a construction company where flair, style, wheeler-dealing skills, speed of decision-making and ability to persuade and to obtain decisions from others were seen as crucial components of a successful entrepreneurial developer. It was said that managers in the development companies did not consider that their progress to the top would be enhanced by a spell on the contracting side.

Because of the close relationships between site managers and their subordinates, and the importance which all companies attach to motivation, which is essentially a downwards influence, it was felt that where managers were not promotable, they should know the company's view and thus have the opportunity to seek work elsewhere. In one or two companies the problem of how to deal with the inevitable situation where promotability is restricted to a small number was resolved by recruitment of a number of site managers for one contract at a time only. In others, as has already been mentioned, personnel were rarely dismissed. Some other job had to be found for them.

8.5.4 External appointment

There are a number of ways of recruiting staff externally and the method adopted depends partly on whether the expertise is required in an area where the company is already operating or in a new type of work. If the company is moving into a new type of work and also if its objective is to grow generally, one course of action is to buy an existing company, primarily to obtain its management though at the same time acquiring its work in hand and other assets. In some cases the company was acquired from the receiver. 'If you want to diversify you do not need to buy a successful company but one with good people and a good name.' There are great risks in proceeding in this way. If the integration of the new company into the existing organisation is not successful the management acquired may well leave to go elsewhere.

The more usual approach is to recruit individuals. It is interesting that in some companies the comment was made that managers from certain other companies would be regarded as being *prima facie* unsuitable for employment because of the different approach to management and the different culture of their present company. An important element in this judgement seemed to be the degree of dependence of other managers on central services as well as the assessment of the overall standard of management within the company for whom the potential recruit was working. Companies prefer to be able to recruit personnel they know well and who, they expect, will integrate easily in the new organisation. Thus some transfer takes place by invitation:

'Recruits from outside are sought from persons known personally for a number of years and not by advertisement'

'It is easy to buy resources in quickly. It is obtaining resources which we can trust and rely on which is difficult.'

If this is not possible then advertisement or 'head-hunting' may be resorted to. There has been an increase in the latter method by which companies commission an employment agency to make enquiries as to who in the industry might be suitable and approach them without initially disclosing the company.

The companies interviewed were wary of their senior managers being 'poached' by others and this has made them more anxious to ensure that their terms and conditions of employment are satisfactory and that they are providing job satisfaction to their managers. The defence against unwelcome head-hunters is to create an environment in which people are comfortable. The least for which senior managers hope is that their managers will discuss an outside offer before accepting.

A number of companies take in school-leavers with O and A levels and train them for site management, expecting them to take ONC and HND. Almost all the companies interviewed regularly recruit young graduates and train them in the company by sending them to courses and by moving them around within the organisation. At the level of recruitment of management trainees, one company has an interesting policy. Because it is easier and cheaper to recruit trainees in the North, the Northern regions are encouraged to recruit and train. The costs of training are borne by the group and allocated to each region according to turnover. This means that the Northern regions can have a higher proportion of trainees without having to bear the cost of training. These trainees can later be employed elsewhere in the group.

There are still senior members of boards of companies who have no degree or equivalent qualification and in building companies senior managers are often surveyors or civil engineers by training rather than building graduates. It should be mentioned that some companies do not really distinguish in their organisation of work between building and civil engineering projects and in such divisions the civil engineers are paramount as managers.

Experiments are in process in the training of graduates and recruits in that at least one company is trying placing them directly in head office jobs rather than giving them initial training on site. In another case graduates are taken from disciplines unconnected with construction and are put through an extensive training period to gain the necessary expertise in construction. Other companies are considering this approach.

It is interesting that while the loss of good senior personnel is fought quite hard by companies, some of them are positively encouraging junior managers to leave and work for another contractor for a while to obtain experience and then having them back again later.

8.5.5 Rewards

Considering that the industry is very decision-intensive (see Section 8.1) and that the value of the contracts and the profits at stake are large, the pay of senior construction managers has been low compared with that in other industries. This situation is beginning to change, first because a number of skills not specific to the construction industry have been brought into the head office staff of contractors – for example, persons to put together major project finance and these have to be paid the going rate right across industry. This has the effect of raising the level of pay of construction staff closer to that offered in other industries. Second, in the boom conditions of 1988 as in upswings generally the rates of pay tend to rise and this is encouraged by the increase in 'head-hunting'. Third, the contracting companies have themselves realised that they need to attract a better calibre of management. Fourth, very senior board-level managers increasingly have a market for their services in commercial client organisations and elsewhere which enables them to command higher remuneration which tends to pull up the general level of managerial salaries. It is of course the total package of remuneration which is important and in more than one company the remuneration of senior personnel included a bonus for good performance. Several companies had some form of profit-sharing scheme.

At the other end of the manager's career the arrangements about retirement are important to him and companies generally now have or are introducing more favourable pension schemes. It is interesting that in a few of the companies interviewed the age of retirement of board members was lower than that of the staff as a whole and in some cases the senior management below board level also had a lower retirement age. The reason is that it is a way of ensuring that younger, energetic staff are at the top of the company and it is also a recognition of the extreme pressure under which these senior persons work.

8.5.6 Training

There was no company which did not undertake some form of training for management personnel. All firms claimed to be very anxious to have good training for their managers but their degree of commitment for the policy and its successful implementation varied from company to company. Though there were some companies where the most senior personnel manager was a member of the group board, in general he was not in the mainstream of activity of the company. This is perhaps strange in an industry which fully recognises the importance of the quality of managers to its success. It is therefore not surprising that dissatisfaction with management training was expressed both by personnel staff and by other senior executives in the companies. In companies where training was well organised there was often someone on the board responsible for all personnel functions. In the majority of companies there was a long-term serious commitment to training and management development, in all parts of the organisation.

In a number of companies the major decisions on personnel matters were taken at subsidiary or regional level so that the personnel manager at head office had at most an advisory and information function. Thus the amount of training given in any part of the organisation is very dependent on the attitude of the manager of that part. This does mean that little is done. One company had a policy of permitting any subsidiaries to train in any way they liked as long as they paid for it and some of the operating units had sent persons to the London Business School to obtain an MBA. In other companies training was a group cost so that it could be undertaken wherever it was most appropriate.

The types of training undertaken included movement from one job to another in order to get experience; and internal and external courses. Movement from job to job within the organisation was very frequently mentioned and is still probably the most important of all types of training. Internal courses covered a variety of approaches from a centre devoted specially to them to taking executives away for a few days to intensive seminars led by senior members of the company or by outsiders. External courses could be specific to the company, specific to the industry or broadly-based management courses. Some of them were run by universities or business centres, including Bradford Senior Executive Development Centre, London Business School, Manchester Business School, Ashridge Management College, Henley Business Centre, Cranfield School, Sheffield Polytechnic and INSEAD (European Institute of Business Administration). The specific subjects mentioned included, for example, purchasing, budgetary control and finance, the last being most frequently mentioned.

The recruitment and training of school leavers with O and A levels and of graduates has been mentioned earlier and the companies which recruit at these levels have comprehensive training schemes of two years or more.

Contractors' main worries concern the more senior training involving the move from site-level management via contract manager to managing a business or participating in that management. Several contractors said that there was a need for management courses and marketing courses internally or externally to ease the transition from site to senior management as discussed in Section 8.5.3 above. It was said that top-level courses were better than they used to be. There is more emphasis on business-environment scenarios so that participants can see the problems of their business in context.

One company has a definite programme of training: at age 28–29 persons with promise are sent to a three-week course at Ashridge. In their mid-30s three or four persons a year go to a business school for a one-month or three-month business course.

In another company, the need to dovetail training to the requirements of individual senior managers was emphasised. 'Training should not be automatic. Every person at a particular level needs a certain amount of training, e.g. a director, in conducting meetings, public speaking, financial appreciation. On the whole, directors are undertrained for their job on the board.'

A warning note was delivered by one director of a company which was active in training. He said:

> the training of senior management is regarded as very important but it is also important to remember that they cannot be trained to be 'street wise' and a well-trained manager who doesn't have the ability to *sense* what he *should* be doing is likely to make major blunders.

In spite of the strong support of this company for training, two problems were mentioned:

(i) if the company faced a rush of orders or serious difficulties on projects then those under training would be taken off their courses;
(ii) some managers were not convinced that it was in their own best interests to be trained.

8.6   OTHER MANAGEMENT ROLES

The discussions on recruitment and development of managers in other parts of the firms brought out sharp differences in attitudes to the employment of non-construction professionals.

In the past two decades, policies of growth and diversification, including the move into foreign markets, has considerably strengthened and broadened the role of senior managers in the finance departments and offered scope for the appointment of professionals not previously connected with the industry. Indeed, it could be claimed that the role of finance director has acquired an aura of importance which is likely to become even brighter as construction companies move more strongly towards acting as principals of the construction process.

Both the need to maximise cash flow from construction itself and to maximise the borrowing facilities to sustain new developments, as well as for skills to organise complicated financial packages have considerably enhanced the status of the finance directors in construction companies. The same is likely to be true of the legal function as defects-liability legislation reaches the statutes book.

Perhaps the fastest growth in managerial posts has been that of information services. The adoption of computers in most companies would seem to have been generally of a piecemeal nature, an internal enthusiastic amateur having taken on the role of early adopter. It certainly does not appear to have often been a matter for board discussion or policy decision. As a result a number of expensive mistakes have been made which are now being rectified by the introduction either of integrated systems or of the installation of interrelated micros. In one or two companies, very sophisticated computer systems have been introduced which in the opinion of some managers, currently offer a range of communications in excess of what they deem practical.

8.7   INNOVATIVE THINKING

The questions on how firms encourage innovative thinking were those where interviewees expressed most surprise and where some had to pause to consider how they wished to reply. As someone put it, 'it was not the type of question submitted by a member of the Stock Exchange'. Indeed the question did not seem to have been formally considered in all companies.

The first obvious answer was that construction work was in itself conducive to innovative thinking since managers were faced with dealing with change, in terms of manpower, skills on site, ground and weather conditions, designers, clients, all of which *per se* demanded a high degree of flexibility, adaptability and innovative responses. One contractor commented that working in the international market generated innovation.

The crucial role of senior managers in motivating their staff and encouraging them to bring forward their ideas for change was also discussed. In some companies there is a fairly formal process for the consideration of ideas for development which goes from the bottom up. In others it is dependent on the individual manager. Planning provides an innovative thinking outlet for some managers.

Efforts to generate innovative thinking are also related to bouts of external training and attendance at seminars and short courses where particular managers would rub shoulders and exchange views with people in similar roles and circumstances in other companies. Setting managers specific projects outside their run-of-the-mill tasks was another way in which one company attempted to encourage innovative thinking.

One of the occasions in which companies not only generate but also monitor new ideas is during the preparation of the five-year plan. This enables all parts of the company to consider at regular intervals where they are heading and how they can develop proposals for development of any particular activity.

Other points mentioned were that non-executive directors were an obvious source of innovative ideas since they were detached from the day-to-day workings of the company and could contribute views developed in other businesses in which they were involved. The executive members of the board sometimes meet outside the normal formal structure of board meetings to discuss longer-term ideas and initiatives. In one or two companies lowering the retirement age of the executive board and bringing in new younger members was seen as one way to promote innovative thinking. It was pointed out that at the bottom of the management hierarchy the new young intake to the company, who had been educated differently from the older managers, would automatically bring with them new views and approaches. It was acknowledged that a policy of internal recruitment made innovative thinking more difficult to achieve.

8.8 ANSWERS TO QUESTIONS POSED BY THEORY

In the companion volume Male and Stocks posed a number of questions to which decision-makers in construction firms should pay particular attention (pp. 104–5). Some of the discussions throw light on how they are considered.

1. *What is the motivation of personnel and the extent to which it might be regarded as appropriate and sufficient?*

Although the survey did not cover this subject it would seem that in an industry where firms are decentralised, most managers would be able to achieve the three goals related to motivation: achievement, affiliation and power. Remuneration however has been low in construction. What would be very interesting is to find the reasons why good school-leavers do not think that the construction industry can provide them with the fulfilment they seek since recruitment of first-class people is still a problem.

2. *Is the definition of roles clear for each person, is the sum of his roles too substantial or too slight a load and is the interrelationship of roles sensible?*

The definition of roles on site is probably adequate and the example of the works manager having to be reminded that he was not in charge of the site is an exception. However, the fact that in this instance certain responsibilities on site were split into administration and supervision suggests that the load on the site manager is very great. The load on directors in some companies is too heavy and attempts have been made to overcome this. Personnel and marketing management roles are not well defined or understood.

3. *Does the company's current system of job appraisal sufficiently utilise the evaluation of performance in roles as a factor in personnel appraisal?*

There are one or two companies where the system functions well. But the short answer must be no. This is one of the aspects of the inadequate emphasis given to the personnel function.

4. *Is there adequate training or other preparation for the assumption by individuals of new roles including the membership of different groups?*

Again the short answer is no. In particular the need for training from site agent to contracts manager and from contracts manager to business manager has been identified.

5. *What is the leadership style appropriate to each function and how far is it matched with the personnel employed in these functions; are the personnel performing better in practice than the theory would suggest and if so why?*

The survey did not provide answers to these questions.

6. *Are there too many or too few formal groups or suborganisations within the company; what are the implications for the work load of senior managers and decision-makers?*

There was a great variation in the number of operating units and of formal committees. It is difficult to say that some had too many and some too few because either could be the structure in equally successful companies. The number of formal groups is closely related to the whole *modus operandi* and therefore it is not possible to make a change in this aspect of the company without consequent parallel changes in other aspects of organisation. For work load see question 2 above and Section 8.4.

7. *Does the representation of particular functions on committees or groups correctly reflect their contribution to the company as a whole?*

There is no evidence that, given the need to keep formal groups small, functions were underrepresented with the exception of personnel and marketing in a number of companies. In some cases individuals had been appointed to boards to give recognition for some efforts rather than because they had an essential function to fulfil.

NOTES AND REFERENCES

1. Male, S. and Stocks, R., 'Managers and the Organisation' in Hillebrandt, P.M. and Cannon, J. (eds) *The Management of Contracting Firms: Aspects of Theory* (London: Macmillan, 1989).
2. See Feldman, D.C. and Arnold, H.J., *Managing Individual and Group Behaviour in Organisations* (Tokyo: McGraw Hill, 1983) and Tichy, N.M., *Managing Strategic Change: Technical, Political and Cultural Dynamics* (New York: Wiley, 1983).
3. Hunt, J.W., *Managing People at Work* (London: McGraw Hill, 1979) pp. 10–13.
4. McClelland, D.C., *The Achieving Society* (Princeton: Van Nostrand, 1961).
5. Handy, C.B., *Understanding Organisations* (Harmondsworth Penguin, 1988).
6. Ibid.

9 Manpower Management and Subcontracting

9.1 INTRODUCTION

There are five characteristics of construction which affect the division of work between that carried out by the contractor himself and that which he contracts out:

1. the finite construction period of each project;
2. the wide geographical spread of location of projects and especially that of large ones which can be undertaken only by major firms;
3. the uneven requirement for specific skills over the life of the project;
4. the wide diversity of skills required is such that any one contractor may not be able to supply all of them;
5. the demand for any particular type of work fluctuates over time.

While the first four derive from the construction process itself, the fifth is the outcome of the investment decisions of businessmen, central and local government and consumers and is inherently different from the other four. These five characteristics together make it very difficult for a contractor to provide all the inputs for a project or to offer continuity of site employment.

For all large projects some of the work is subcontracted to other specialist firms (some of which may be subsidiaries of the main contractor) which take full responsibility for undertaking a package of work including the supply of materials, known as supply-and-fix subcontracting.

After the Second World War the provision of work for operatives was organised by means of a small labour force in continuous employment by construction firms complemented with employment on a casual basis for the remainder of the labour force. The casual nature of employment in the industry was indeed a matter of concern to some unions and to policy-makers in the early 1960s.[1] This method of employment was gradually replaced by labour-only subcontracting

137

which is now the predominant method of obtaining labour in the south of the country and increasingly so elsewhere.

The subject of subcontracting is one where there is virtual unanimity in the views of the contractors interviewed, with the actual decisions on the employment of labour-only subcontractors left entirely to the discretion of the site manager who is expected to be fully aware of the demand and supply conditions of the local labour market.

9.2   SUPPLY-AND-FIX SUBCONTRACTING

The extent of supply-and-fix subcontracting is partly determined by the type of work the firm offers. The narrower its span the more it will need to subcontract. Other reasons for using subcontractors include short-term overload in the firm, inconvenient geographical location of a project or lack of specialist capability.

Typical of the services which are obtained from supply-and-fix subcontractors are those with highly specialised skill, materials or plant, such as electrical, heating and ventilating services; site investigation; piling, plumbing and roofing. It is not unusual in a high-quality commercial building to have a ratio of cost of services to cost of building of 60:40. At one extreme the main contractor may do very little work himself even if he is working on a traditional contract as distinct from a form of management contract. At the other extreme the services contractor may be the main contractor with the building part subcontracted.

The use of subcontractors does not necessarily simplify the management of the main contractor although it shifts some of the risk on to the subcontractor. Moreover, because many of the subcontracts have a clause which stipulates that the subcontractor will be paid only after the main contractor is paid by the client, the cash flow of the main contractor is enhanced.

9.3   LABOUR-ONLY SUBCONTRACTING

9.3.1   Definition and extent of use

Labour-only subcontracting is a broad term to describe the situation in which the contractor arranges for an operative group or individual to agree to work on his project while retaining self-employed status. A labour-only subcontractor may be part of a gang or working as a single individual; he may be employed on piece-rate or by time-rate; he may be recruited directly or through an agency. Most of the contractors interviewed employ labour-only subcontractors in groups, sometimes operating as limited companies, on piece-rates and recruited directly. They are used both on building and civil engineering contracts. Resort to the use of agency-recruited personnel on an hourly or daily rate is made in emergency situations only. Nevertheless some contractors employ labour-only subcontractors with whom they have worked on a time-rate basis and it is common practice for contractors to employ the same subcontractors again and again so that they are almost part of their permanent team.

Several contractors differentiated between the use of labour-only subcontractors in the north and south of the country. In the south they are used extensively with almost all the labour force being engaged on this basis though most firms prefer to keep a core of their own directly employed operatives, particularly those with special or high-quality skills as well as a range of skills to be available immediately as required. Other contractors said that their own policy was the same in the north and the south but there was a preference by major public clients in the north for work to be carried out as far as possible by directly employed labour and this policy has the full support of local trade union officials. As a consequence, in the north, especially in Scotland, there is still more directly employed labour but in northern England labour-only subcontracting is spreading.

One contractor thought that it was not so much geographical location which determined the amount of subcontracted labour but the size and type of project – large and sophisticated projects normally having a high level of subcontracting. Since most large building projects are in the south the two views are not incompatible.

It is obvious that it is only when a firm has an order-book which guarantees continuous employment within a defined area for the main range of skills for a relatively long period and where it is confident about prospects beyond this period, that its direct labour force can look forward to a stable spell of employment. The larger the type of project in which the firm engages, the less likely stable employment becomes. A lengthy period of regional growth thus offers the best opportunities for continuous employment; sharp and short booms the worst.

A contractor who uses a high proportion of subcontractors nevertheless said that he tried to use much of his own directly employed labour on renovation work because it was more difficult to define the work to be done on piece-work and because it was necessary to know the capabilities of the craftsmen.

Not only main contractors but also supply-and-fix subcontractors use labour-only subcontractors – for example, for extremely specialised tasks and to cope with peaks of workload so that they can keep their own workforce at a constant level. Where very high quality work is involved and also, most importantly, where work is dangerous subcontractors would normally use their own labour – for example, in scaffolding, asbestos removal and demolition. Main contractors employing such supply-and-fix subcontractors will vet their safety record very carefully.

Incidentally, for specialist trades it sometimes happens that contractors borrow labour from their competitors to deal with peaks in workload.

9.3.2   Overall advantages and disadvantages

(a)   The theoretical approach

In the chapter on manpower management by Buckley and Enderwick in the companion volume the approach adopted to the analysis of the choice between labour-only subcontracting and direct employment is based on the distinction between the internal labour market (ILM) (that is, internal to the organisation) and the external contract for the employment of labour.[2] The internal labour market is linked to theories of hierarchical organisations developed by Williamson and others. The theoretical approach leads to the conclusion that there should have been a movement towards the internal labour market and away from subcontracting. In fact the importance of the internal labour market has declined probably ever since the end of the Second World War. The explanations given by Buckley and Enderwick for the decline in the internal labour market lie in the characteristics of the construction industry (Sections 8.3.3 and 8.3.4 of Chapter 8) and are summarised below:

1. output fluctuations lead to a preference for short duration contracts including those for labour and the shift of risk to labour in the form of self-employment and dependent subcontracting;
2. the craft nature of labour means that it is not machine-paced and hence less amenable to control by management;

3. in spite of the low density of union membership the constraints imposed by unions may well have been instrumental in pushing employers away from the internal labour contract.

Buckley and Enderwick then go on to say that the benefits of subcontracting may well encompass control attributes:

> While management has never been able fully to control the craft-based work process in construction, their influence may be enhanced where subcontracting is prevalent. Firstly, such a mode creates dual dependence; the worker depends on the subcontractor for his wage while employment opportunities are the domain of the principal contractor. Secondly, the system proved efficient in responding to labour shortages in the 1960s. Subcontracting allowed earnings to be bid up when demand required but such increases were never consolidated through collective bargaining. Thirdly, the opportunities for increased earnings discouraged reliance on construction unions and fostered self-employment. Fourthly, subcontracting strengthened both horizontal and vertical hierarchy of workers causing division within the workforce. The coexistence of workers employed by different firms, under different terms and arrangements and for varying durations weakens labour cohesion and the identification of mutual interest[3] (pp. 119, reference number altered).

It was found in the survey that the inefficient features of subcontracting found in manufacturing industry are attenuated in construction.

Another major reason why the theoretical analysis would not have been able to predict what has happened in construction lies in the nature of the choice in construction. It is not really the choice between labour-only subcontracting and a stable permanent directly employed labour force whose employment is regulated by collective agreements and organised in a hierarchical way. If it were, some of the potential advantages of the internal market spelt out in theory might obtain. They were described as follows:

> When individual contracts are replaced by a general collective agreement, the rigidity of the authority relationship is reduced. Furthermore, peer group involvement increases the likelihood of a constructive response to change. The substitution of a collective agreement for a series of individual contracts stresses the import-

ance of organisational interests over individual concerns and re-
duces the incentives for opportunistic behaviour. The assignment
of wage rates to tasks as opposed to individuals serves to increase
flexibility.

The incentive group structure of the ILM facilitates efficient
internal exchange. A promotional/reward system based on seniority fosters cooperation and the sharing of task-specific knowledge.
Screening can be achieved at a lower cost and risks can be reduced
when entry to the group occurs mainly at lower level positions.
Such an arrangement also discourages labour turnover since the
loss of seniority and other pecuniary rights are a disincentive to
mobility. The system is strengthened when self-monitoring of
groups is encouraged and internal methods of conflict resolution
are set up (p. '112).

This does not ring true of construction at all except possibly for
management. That is because the real choice is between labour-only
subcontracting and a series of *ad hoc* casual temporary employments
where the gang has to be organised anew for each contract and where
the individuals employed have virtually no concern for the organisation because they are only temporarily linked to it. Certainly contractors always had a permanent internal labour force which was
shifted from site to site. But most of them still do. As was said in one
company:

'We would prefer to employ our own labour directly and we regard
it as essential to keep a core of trained personnel in direct employment.'

In another company, in relation to a specialised field of work, it
was said

'only by doing a good job, that is, by using our own labour, can we
keep our reputation'.

(b)   The contractors' views

The main advantages of subcontracting were discussed in terms of
reduced costs, increased efficiency and speed of work, when compared with direct employment. It is worth noting that those interviewed were all of the opinion that subcontracting had lower costs
overall than direct employment, but there had been no attempt to

justify their views by a formal assessment of the two alternatives as the firms felt they often had no choice.

The decision on the method of employment was seen as determined by the condition of the local labour market.

'We have no central policy on labour because the right commercial decisions have to be made at the local level.'

'Employment policy is left to the man who is going to do the job.'

'The pub provides good market intelligence.'

'Foremen and site managers have their own following. They refer to *my* brickies, *my* joiners.'

The efficiency advantages are of two types, first, those related directly to costs and to productivity (see Section 9.3.3) and, second, that because of the concentration on projects geographically dispersed it is impractical for large contractors to offer any great continuity of employment. The existence of the labour-only subcontracting network enables them to obtain specialist labour gangs quickly wherever and whenever they need them. Conversely by working for many contractors in an area the labour-only subcontractors can obtain sufficient work without excessive travelling.[4]

Taken together these factors mean that the use of subcontracting is the most profitable short-term solution for contractors and, in addition, the price competition on a separate basis for each project means that this is the solution which has to be adopted even if a contractor feels that, in the long run and in order to do the best work, he would prefer more direct employment. Indeed almost all firms claim that they would prefer to have a larger directly employed labour force than they currently have. This is particularly true of those firms which hark back to the close relationships between owners and employees in earlier times.

The main disadvantages were related to the longer-term impact of great reliance on subcontractors and in particular on its adverse impact on the availability and level of skills of the labour force. Others are risk and lack of control. One company which tries hard to employ labour directly is very concerned at the use of labour-only subcontractors. It was said that:

Labour-only subcontracting results in inadequate training, unsatisfactory employment conditions and inadequate control over

labour. As in the industry generally, the group has a fair proportion of directly employed labour in the north and west of the
country, though even there the balance is shifting towards subcontracting, and in the south it mainly uses subcontractors, employing
directly only few of the key tradesmen. The reason for the use of
subcontracting is the intense price competition in the industry
which dictates that the most profitable short-term solution shall be
used.

Without exception, all firms expressed worry at the current training situation, especially as it concerns trades and supervisory levels.
During the past one and a half decades, a decreasing workload led
firms to cut back severely on their intake of trainees and it is in any
case difficult to train with a low direct labour force. When order
books began to fill up again labour-only subcontracting increased and
there is little incentive for labour-only subcontractors to undertake
training.

All firms interviewed referred to their support for good training
and take in some young apprentices but it is the subcontracted skills,
where they are unable to exercise the necessary control, which
worries them most. In some cases they have reached agreement with
subcontractors whereby the latter undertake to take on trainees on
behalf of the main contractors.

Although both employers and employees are represented on CITB
committees there was widespread dissatisfaction expressed on a
number of current training policies and activities of the CITB and in
particular the slow and inadequate response of the CITB to the
deep-seated changes which have taken place in the industry in the
past decade. The increase in the share of building services in the total
cost of modern commercial premises has in no way been matched by
an adequate increase in the number of apprentices to the relevant
trades, nor has the CITB given sufficient attention to the different
levels of workload and mix of workload in the regions. Where praise
was given it tended to refer to some of the training programmes
offered at Bircham Newton, such as those for scaffolders.

There is a variety of in-house training activities in all firms which
were visited. These ranged from the relatively informal sessions,
mainly relying on inputs by senior managers of the firm, to formal
external courses at colleges. A number of interviewees mentioned
the considerable contribution to training at YTS level by two of the
larger firms in the industry.

Another factor to be considered in the pros and cons of the two methods of employment is the risk element. When the subcontractors work to a well-defined price the main contractor is able to shed some risk – for example, some of the risk arising from bad weather. This advantage, however, is tempered by the danger of subcontractors going into liquidation if the price is too keen and the contractor will prefer a reliable less cheap subcontractor to the cheapest untried one. As one contractor said:

> The risk of employing our own labour is generally regarded as higher, although we often do get problems with subcontractors going bust during the contract and this seems to happen more often with civil engineering contracts, especially muck-shifting. Because of the danger of subcontractors going out of business, we do not necessarily accept the lowest tender.

A further factor is the relative powerlessness of main contractors to deal with delays by subcontractors. The additional costs borne by the firm because of failure on the part of subcontractors to undertake work as agreed include the knock-on effects on activities further along the building process. The crucial importance of ensuring that subcontractors meet the requirements of the main contractors for whom they work has led one large firm to consider as an inducement offering the subcontractor's workforce fringe benefits akin to those available to its own labour force.

9.3.3   Costs of labour-only subcontracting

Contractors take into account, and discussed during the interviews, direct costs, administrative costs and costs of management. The theory considers direct costs of all types, and in recent years has highlighted transaction costs – that is, the cost involved in buying and selling both goods and services including manpower. The chapter by Buckley and Enderwick in the companion volume highlights transaction costs particularly in relation to the choice between the internal and external labour contract. These are largely the administrative costs discussed by contractors. Each of the types of costs considered by contractors is discussed separately below.

(a)   Direct costs

The direct costs of labour only are the amounts paid under the contract agreed on a piece-rate basis or the amounts due under time-rate. The rates vary according to the demand and supply position in the labour market. When there is a boom in construction as, for example, in 1973 or 1988, rates become very high and then fall again in periods of low workload.

The direct cost of directly employed labour is more complicated. The rate negotiated between the trade unions and the employers' organisations is very low compared with both the actual earnings especially in a period of boom, and the direct costs of the labour-only subcontractors. However, the bonus payments are very substantial and the employer must also pay national insurance contributions, sick pay and holiday stamps.

The real direct costs need to take account of productivity. It is generally believed that productivity of labour-only subcontractors on piece work is higher than that of directly employed labour where the incentive is less. No hard evidence is available; indeed it would be difficult to obtain because the directly employed labour and the labour-only subcontractors are now usually employed on quite different tasks in different circumstances. However, one contractor commented that:

> The cost of labour-only compared with direct employment depends on the current market for labour-only subcontractors. If the work is done on a piece-work basis it may be cheaper and is a way of reducing tenders, e.g. drainage contractors on civil engineering work. In estimating in our company the job is priced on the basis of own labour costs and productivity and this has been found to be about right for labour-only subcontracting too.

There is another direct cost of employment of directly employed persons and that is the redundancy payment under the Employment Protection Act, 1975. The fact that redundancy payments are not payable for less than two years employment is not very helpful because the unions insist on a policy of last in, first out, so that any major restructuring which involves a large part of any workforce is bound to involve substantial payments. There are also administrative costs.

(b) Administrative costs

It is desirable to compare the administrative costs of using labour-only subcontractors both with a directly employed permanent workforce and with a casual workforce as used in the 1950s and 1960s.

The ways labour-only subcontractors are obtained are (i) by telephoning subcontractors well-known to the company to discuss availability and terms (this is the preferred way); (ii) by using an agency; (iii) by visiting public houses well-known as a labour market. If the first is successful the administrative costs may be very small as also in method (ii). The last is likely to be more costly in time and beer. However in all cases once the subcontractors are located the costs of settling the fairly standard arrangements are low.

If the firm manages to keep its operatives for some time the recruitment – often by recommendation or some advertisement – of directly employed personnel will be fairly low when spread over the total cost of labour. In earlier years the recruitment of a casual labour force was also at low cost. If there was a shortage of work operatives toured sites to see where there were vacancies, but in a time of shortage of operations of operatives the labour exchange and the public house were used.

The administrative costs of directly employed labour are high. They include computing and paying wages, bonuses, other benefits and then deducting national insurance and PAYE, and dealing with operatives' complaints and queries on their pay. These costs would arise with permanent and also with casual directly employed men. The comparable costs for the self-employed are those of arranging the contract. Sometimes this is an informal arrangement but several contractors who were interviewed use only formal contracts as a matter of policy.

Another administrative cost associated with the direct employment of manpower is the paper work associated with the Employment Protection Act, 1975. This includes informing the Department of Employment that redundancies have taken place. These complications do not of course arise with the self-employed.

The conclusion that administrative costs are considerably higher for directly employed (internal) labour than for labour-only subcontracting is contrary to the expectations of the theory.[5] This is partly because the work of any employee in construction varies considerably within site and between sites which together with the complex pay structure means that the administration of the payments to him and the potential for dispute are substantial with consequent high costs.

(c) Management costs

The broad advantages and disadvantages to the firm of the various types of employment and contracting of labour have been dealt with in Section 9.3.2 above. It seems appropriate here to consider the specific point of whether the costs of supervision and management of the workforce are greater with direct employment or labour-only subcontracting. Different views emerged in discussions with contractors. Some thought that the piece-work payment system often used implied the need for a much greater degree of supervision to control the natural wish to finish the work as quickly as possible at the expense of quality. No contractor regarded the degree of supervision required as substantially less than for directly employed labour and most regarded it as roughly the same. As one contractor put it:

> The amount of management with labour-only subcontractors is not less than with the employment of own labour because the firm is still just as responsible for the job and therefore for its proper execution.

9.3.4   The labour-only subcontractors' point of view

The views of the contractors on their lack of choice in the use of labour-only subcontractors are partly borne out by evidence from other sources. The Phelps Brown committee report pointed out some of the advantages (and disadvantages) to the operatives,[6] and the OPCS survey into *Labour Mobility in the Construction Industry* quoted extensively from interviews with operatives in which they expressed a strong preference for self employment.[7] The growth of labour-only subcontracting in the south of the country in a period of expanding workload suggests that in this suppliers' market the operatives have opted strongly for labour-only subcontracting. The reasons may be summarised as follows:

1. more independence including a choice of when they will work and on what type and location of work;
2. higher take home pay;
3. potential for charging certain expenses against tax, e.g. car and telephone which they might have had anyway. Moreover tax and national insurance are paid after a period of delay. It may also be that some earnings are not declared.

There are of course disadvantages of self-employment as follows:

1. risk that work will not be available, especially as unemployment benefit is not payable;

2. greater administration (the transaction costs fall on them not the employer);
3. risk that rates of pay will fall considerably in a downturn in the industry;
4. risk of sickness, as no sickness benefit is paid.

In fact, apart from the greater administration, which also contributes to the feeling of independence, and the risk of illness which is insurable, disadvantages arise only in a downturn in the industry. In a situation where training in the industry is at a dangerously low level the good labour-only subcontractor should be able to find work even in a downturn and many contractors think that it is the best craftsmen who have become self-employed.

In these circumstances it is perhaps correct that the contractors feel that they are pushed into using labour-only subcontractors because they are the principal supply of manpower available in the marketplace. This contrasts sharply with the theory which concentrates on the demand side. It may also explain some of the contradictions on the demand side. Though most contractors think that labour-only subcontracting is cheaper, they almost all wish there were less of it. All feel they have little choice. The fact that the operatives themselves are not prepared to make themselves available at the prices ruling in the market for directly employed work for the reasons given above means that at least when the industry wants their services in large quantities because construction is booming the contractors really have little choice. In order to swing back the trend towards direct employment quite dramatic changes would be necessary in the pay and conditions of direct employment. These are unlikely to be on a scale sufficient to have the necessary impact. Labour-only subcontracting seems to be here to stay for the foreseeable future.

NOTES AND REFERENCES

1. *Report of the Committee of Inquiry under Professor E.H. Phelps Brown into Certain Labour in Building and Civil Engineering*, 3714 (London: HMSO 1968), para 231.
2. Buckley, J. and Enderwick, P., 'Manpower Management' in Hillebrandt, P.M., and Cannon, J. (eds) *The Management of Large Construction Firms: Aspects of Theory* (London: Macmillan, 1989) ch. 8. This source is often quoted and is indicated by page or section numbers.
3. Villa P, 'Labour Market Segmentation in the Construction Industry in Italy' in Wilkinson, F. (ed.) *The Dynamics of Labour Market Segmentation* (London: Academic Press, 1981).

4. It should be noted in passing that the important factor is time, not distance. All over the country an hour is regarded as reasonable travelling time. In London this may be equal to say 4 or 5 miles, in Yorkshire or Scotland to 50–60 miles.
5. Buckley and Enderwick see note 2.
6. Phelps Brown Committee Report see Note 1, paras 393–409.
7. Marsh, A., Heady, P. and Matheson, J., *Labour Mobility in the Construction Industry*, OPCS (London: HMSO, 1981).

Part V
Conclusions

10 Conclusions

This chapter is in three distinct parts. In the first, each subject area is discussed in a summarised form, which emphasises those aspects of the strategies of large firms where a great degree of similarity or diversity was met. The second part focuses on the relationship between construction firms' actual operation and the theoretical ideas propounded in the companion volume.[1] The third part is concerned with those areas where further research and analytical work or new endeavours are required.

10.1 STRATEGY AND BEHAVIOUR

The companies visited had turnovers which ranged from about £100 million to a considerable multiple of that sum. The ownership of firms fell into three categories: family-controlled, subsidiaries of large corporations and other public limited companies. As might be expected, there were similar patterns of behaviour and reactions to external circumstances across all companies. Where there were differences in behaviour or performance, these could often be related to the particular form of company.

The study was most opportune in that the fall in domestic contracting work from 1973 had forced construction firms to rethink their strategies. Later, with the decline in overseas markets, they had had to review their operations abroad. The results are now becoming evident. One or two contractors had left this process rather late and have been belatedly forced by poor results to examine their strategy. Others had taken costly wrong decisions in certain areas. However, the overall impression gained is one of greater concern with tight management and improved levels of efficiency than at any time in the post-war period.

Discussions on the broad strategic approach adopted by the firms in the survey indicate an unexpected diversity, both as regards their understanding of the meaning of strategy and the manner in which it was developed and implemented. There was a widespread confusion between the interpretation of strategy, objectives and planning, both between companies and within companies among quite senior members of staff. Chapter 2, by Ramsay in the companion volume,[2] has much to offer in this respect and in a matter of such importance as the framework for the firm's future development, many companies, both large and not so large, would benefit from a clear understanding of the three concepts, mission, strategy and objectives.

All firms had suffered from the recession but not all gave the same attention to refocusing their policy. Those which did were helped by the Middle East boom and took advantage of the breathing space which it gave them to redevelop their strategy. They were all affected by the decline of public-sector demand from the mid-1970s and most attempted to diversify into other types of construction work and away from civil engineering. Those firms which responded only belatedly to the changed market situation tended to fall within the category of family-controlled firms which, as previous chapters have shown, are affected by circumstances not met within non-family firms and which, by and large, inhibit change. It remains a remarkable fact that such a large proportion of the top thirty-five firms belong to that group.

Major reasons why families have been able to retain control in contracting (as opposed to manufacturing) firms are that contracting requires very low fixed assets and is cash-generating so that the families have not needed to raise capital to expand their contracting businesses. With the increasing trend toward diversification of company activities into capital-intensive operations, this is becoming more difficult to sustain. Moreover, in some businesses the family's ownership of the shares is becoming increasingly remote from the managers. There may well be a decrease in the level of family control.

The examination of strategy was usually undertaken by the board itself. Though consultants were employed to advise on specific problems, with one or two exceptions companies were not keen on asking consultants to undertake full strategic reviews. All companies were well aware of the danger of growth of turnover without a parallel increase in profits because they had been hit by the low margins of the late 1970s and early 1980s.

At the time of the interviews nearly all companies were seeking further opportunities for diversification or, in a few cases, consolidating recent acquisitions. Contracting firms have long diversified into areas related to their core business such as property development and speculative housing, which are capital-intensive and provide a profitable outlet for the cash generated by contracting operations. However, in the last decade or so there has been a major diversification into businesses very different from contracting such as mining, scientific instruments and materials merchanting. These activities require a large amount of capital which far exceeds that available from contracting operations. Contracting has ceased to be a dominant activity in some construction companies and, in the event of another major downturn in demand, this trend would be intensified. In determining what diversification they should undertake, construction firms look for activities which do not follow normal construction cycles and where they have some know-how which they can utilise.

Diversification was not an option equally available to the three groups of firms. The public limited companies would encounter least difficulties in diversifying. The family firms had problems in raising funds without diluting their financial interests, and, for subsidiaries of large corporations, diversification could be a closed door. Whatever the type of company there were two different approaches to diversification. In the one case it was a carefully planned operation with deliberate preferences in terms of type, size and location of business. In the other case diversification was thought to be a good thing but was not pursued in a purposeful manner so that companies considered opportunities only as they presented themselves.

Though all firms now do some planning, there are major differences in the type and extent of planning activities undertaken by construction firms. With very few exceptions, financial budgeting is fairly well organised and sometimes it is regarded as synonymous with planning. The latter is increasingly undertaken, not necessarily with much conviction. Moreover, the knowledge of the plans is often not widely disseminated which would seem partly to invalidate the exercise. It is not possible to say that firms which appear to plan best are necessarily the most efficient. It is notable, however, that most of the firms interviewed which have recently had major problems in their operations have only just started planning (often as a result of their difficulties) or had poorly developed planning systems.

Where financial policy in construction firms differs from that in firms in other industries is in the positive contribution to cash flow which can be and should be made by the contracting side of the business. All firms fully recognised this crucial aspect of financial policy though in one or two cases its full implications had only recently been appreciated and action to take advantage of the benefits had been slow.

Where contractors are part of a conglomerate the control of the latter over day-to-day operations of the contracting subsidiary is slight. The main motive for owning a contracting firm is financial, especially the positive cash flow, though in some cases there is also a link with other activities of the conglomerate – for example, property development.

In a well-diversified business with a balanced portfolio it is easier to raise external funds and the less diversified firms with lower capital assets obviously face more difficulties in raising finance than the others. Quite apart from the ability to raise funds, the attitudes of some firms constrain their willingness to borrow and hence their prospects for growth and diversification. The degree of risk-aversion in contracting differs greatly from one company to another and it affects in particular attitudes to growth and diversification because of its financial implications.

Indeed, the objectives of all firms were primarily financial and the need to look after shareholders' interests was often mentioned. In part, the acute awareness of financial objectives is related to the need to keep a close watch on the price of the company's shares, and to try to ensure that the company is well regarded by analysts. The valuation of the company by the stock market is carefully monitored because of its effect on the likelihood of takeover.

In family-controlled firms, it is obvious that external pressure on performance, particularly from the Stock Exchange, is far less significant than in other companies. Family shareholders are constrained from selling their shares for fear of losing control, and they are therefore less concerned than other shareholders with profit maximisation or capital growth. What matters to them is that dividends, which may be their main source of income, should be maintained at a reasonable level, after allowing for the effects of inflation and taxation.

Marketing is by far the weakest function in the construction firms visited and that which is most in need of attention by policy-makers. All firms are aware of the importance of marketing which has been forced upon them by the retrenchment of the public-sector client. However, few firms have developed an effective marketing capability. Many are still floundering towards the development of a marketing policy and the means to implement and integrate it into the company's other activities. The exception is in the international contracting field where the nature of the client and the scale and glamour of projects often require understanding of marketing and the use of more sophisticated marketing tools and techniques.

It is not surprising that because of the various attitudes to risk, it was found that some firms were more conservative than others in their approach to bidding and relied on various mechanisms to ensure that the operations side of the business did not exceed its limits of authority. Implicitly they were relying on the opportunity cost approach to determine the boundaries to bidding. It might be helpful to them to become better acquainted with the principles.

There have been substantial changes in the international contracting markets, including the recent considerable fall in the level of work on offer. Contractors are also finding it increasingly difficult to compete with those from semi-industrialised countries in one-off contracts. There are many problems in continuing as a large 'local' contractor in developing countries. Many contractors have allowed their international operations to shrink, though few wish to pull out altogether. By contrast, contracting firms are moving into other geographical markets, notably the USA, and into non-contracting activities. Some also operate in Europe though the attitude is one of great wariness in committing themselves to European contracting operations.

It was in their organisation and structure that the large firms were found to be most dissimilar. When attempts are made to relate the particular forms of organisation and structure adopted by them to their standards of performance, it is not possible to conclude that any one form is better than another. Even though in many cases their structures were the outcome of well-considered deliberations, they all appeared to accept that changes might be necessary in the future.

The degree of control exercised by the main board over the activities of the firm at subsidiary levels varies greatly from one company to another. Some have tight supervision and control accompanied by a high level of central services. Others have loose control mechanisms except in financial matters. Each is said to work well where it operates. Some companies rely heavily on committees and others are proud that they have none. The general philosophy and method of working of the company are part of its culture. It is difficult to transfer a culture and this has caused problems in certain mergers.

It is obvious that the communications system needs to be compatible with the organisational structure but little attention appears to have been explicitly given to it. As a result in some cases communication networks seem poorly organised. The lack of a homogeneous policy on communication was highlighted in the haphazard introduction of computer systems. In a number of cases, failure to adopt a policy towards information technology at board level had led to the adoption of unrelated *ad hoc* systems and to costly mistakes. At least one company introduced a comprehensive system. Poor communications could also be due to insufficient awareness by policy-makers of what information should be imparted up and down the line and how best to do it.

All senior managers interviewed were fully aware of the importance of human resources and especially of management. Their awareness contrasted strongly with the fact that in a number of companies personnel functions and roles seemed inadequate to the task. This may be partly because management in the industry is still essentially a matter of people-management and because the personnel role is considered more in advisory terms than in policy terms. As a result less attention is paid to some of the fundamentals of personnel policy, such as training and the development of management, than would seem compatible with the needs of this type of industry. There is great diversity in the extent to which manpower planning is undertaken and some companies have not adequately planned the succession of top posts.

The nature of the contracting industry means that direct long-term employment of labour for all work is not possible for large contractors undertaking major contracts widely dispersed throughout the country. Labour-only subcontracting has largely replaced casual direct employment as the means of overcoming this problem. It is seen by contractors as being more cost-effective than direct employment and there is evidence that some of the workforce prefers it. In spite of the fact that contractors believe that it is more cost-effective in the short run, there is some dissatisfaction with it mainly because of a lack of suitable training mechanisms and because of the difficulty of overcoming the resistance of some unions and some clients. Contractors do not have any alternative in reality to using labour-only subcontractors, especially in the south of the country, and all parties to the construction process would do well to recognise that labour-only subcontracting is here to stay and the construction industry as a whole should devote its energies to removing the disadvantages of the system.

There has also been a movement towards more supply-and-fix subcontracting, partly because of the growth in management contracting. This also brings problems of lack of training of skilled operatives, mainly employed in subcontracted trades.

10.2   RELATIONSHIP TO THEORY

The purpose of the companion volume was to make available to practitioners in the construction industry – whether professionals or managers – some of the up-to-date thinking of experts in the managerial sciences on the contribution of their subjects relevant to the contracting industry. It was one of the purposes of interviews with contractors reported in this volume to discover the extent to which these ideas were known to managers in contracting firms and the extent to which managers were acting in accordance with them.

The behaviour of many of those interviewed was consistent with some of the precepts of theory, notably some aspects of the overall formulation of strategy, diversification, international, financial and pricing policy. There are two explanations for managers' behaviour which does not accord with the theories outlined in the companion volume. The first is lack of knowledge of the relevant concepts by managers. The second is lack of relevance of the theory to the organisation, structure and behaviour of construction firms.

In the first case most managers in contracting firms were unaware of much of the potential contribution of economics, management science, sociology and other disciplines to the improvement of management. There were some exceptions. The ideas developed by Handy in *Understanding Organisations* were acknowledged as was the Boston matrix (see Chapters 2 and 5).[3,4] In another company the Chief Executive had distributed a copy of *In Search of Excellence* to all senior managers.[5]

More generally, the survey conducted in large firms demonstrated that there is a number of areas where greater awareness, or knowledge of current theoretical writings would be of benefit to managers. There are too few firms where a well-developed and systematic approach has been set in place to ensure that managers, as distinct from professionals, are kept abreast of up-to-date thinking.

In the second case, the ideas developed in the companion volume are neither equally theoretical nor equally applicable. They may be divided into three groups.

The first group consists of those subjects where an answer to the question 'What should I do?' is possible. These are notably those covered in the chapter by Ramsay.[6] The answer is that objectives should be formulated, a strategy developed, planning undertaken. The chapter does not say what the strategy should be but suggests ways of approaching the problems. In this volume it was found that it is accepted that a strategy should be developed and operations planned but that there is a long way to go in determining methods and effective implementation. Ideas in Ramsay's chapter should be widely disseminated.

The second group provides a logical framework of the relevant factors in the choice between various options. Thus the chapter by Cannon and Hillebrandt dealing with diversification does not say that firms should diversify but points out the types of diversification, the advantages and disadvantages and the circumstances in which various types might be beneficial.[7] To a firm contemplating diversification this analytical approach would be helpful in formulating policy in a logical manner.

Another chapter which falls into this broad category is that on international policy by Seymour.[8] The theory of multinational enterprises seems to come closer to the practice of construction firms than do many other elements of theory. The chapter on finance by Cannon and Hillebrandt shows how some of the precepts applicable to most of industry are less relevant to decision making in contracting firms.[9] It provides a useful checklist of factors which should be considered in financial policy. Both these chapters select aspects of theory which are generally applicable to industry as a whole and consider their relevance to construction.

The last chapter in this category is that on management and the organisation by Male and Stocks,[10] whose approach is broader and consists of setting out a range of ideas which they consider relevant to managers' behaviour and to the type of organisation in which they function. There is little which is prescriptive but questions are raised as to whether there is scope for improvement in firms' behaviour.

The third group deals with aspects of corporate and human activity and implicitly invites a comparison with practice. The relevant chapters include the most difficult ideas for the manager to use. They are the most theoretical and hence may be considered the furthest removed from the day-to-day preoccupations of many managers. Together they offer the opportunity for a more rigorous insight into management theories than is readily available to construction managers.

The chapter on pricing policy by Flanagan and Norman outlines a methodology of price determination which takes into account factors not normally considered in the more mechanistic bidding theories.[11]

In the chapter on structure and organisation Clark selects a theory

based on the social-technology approach and highlights the importance of the level and stability of information in determining appropriate organisational structures.[12] Some of the difficulties encountered
in applying this particular approach to construction firms are highlighted in chapter 7 of this volume. By deliberately focusing on a
single theoretical model Clark has offered a challenging opportunity
to test its relevance to construction firms in a more detailed manner
than is possible with more broadly based chapters. Inevitably however his approach precludes any comparison between the relevance
of his selected approach and that of other theories.

Lastly in the chapter on manpower management the argument
developed by Buckley and Enderwick is based on the theories of the
internal labour market and hierarchical organisations and applies
them to the problem of labour-only subcontracting.[13] It is found that
the theory does not satisfactorily explain practice. Buckley and
Enderwick attempt to explain the discrepancies by reference to the
specific characteristics of construction. Part of the explanation may
lie in the concentration of the theory on the demand side to the
exclusion of the supply side.

The first group of chapters 'What should be done and how?' and
much of the second group – 'Have all the relevant factors and their
effects been taken into consideration and assessed?' are obvious
material for senior management courses, in postgraduate teaching
and in some cases for undergraduate teaching. They are also addressed
to directors and senior managers in construction companies. The third
group is for selective use. These chapters are more likely to provide a
basis for further investigations or a useful intellectual framework for
senior executives involved in the development of longer-term policies
such as revamping the organisational structure, of overhauling the
bidding policies or of improving the company performance by improving the quality of manpower. They are less suitable for broadly
based management courses.

10.3   THE WAY FORWARD

When we were seeking contributions for the companion volume it
became obvious that in the academic world at large there is very little
interest in the analysis of the operation of the contracting or construction industry, let alone a body of research or knowledge with the
construction industry as its central focus. Funding of research,

whether from public or private sources, has been essentially ear-marked for technical matters and, if for management, mainly at site level. Yet this volume has shown that the nature of the construction business and particularly the contracting business is very different from that of manufacturing and it is clear from much of the analysis that the management strategy of the firm is vital to performance. Academics would do a service to the construction industry and to the development of their subject areas by becoming more deeply in-volved in the management of construction at the level of the firm. Some of the chapters on theory would have been more relevant had their writers had a more intimate knowledge of the way the industry operates.

At the same time the relevance of some of the existing theory to the management strategy of the industry has also been demonstrated. Most managerial posts in the industry are held by professionals who would benefit from a broader perspective. Large firms should im-prove their relations with academic researchers – for instance, by inviting them to discuss their work with managers or by sending managers on courses which would broaden and deepen their knowl-edge. There is one particular area in which most senior managers declared a strong wish to be better informed, namely finance. More people should be encouraged to take greater advantage of the financial courses on offer than appears to be the case.

A major problem is that there is no centre for all the disciplines relevant to the construction industry. Given the crucial importance of the management resource to the well-being of the industry there is an urgent need for large firms to give active and lasting support to the establishment of a centre of excellence where all the aspects of research relevant to management in the industry could be brought together. One of the functions of such a centre would be to ensure that the results of research were more widely available to those who might benefit from them.

Both this book and the companion volume have established the potential contribution of theory to the behaviour and performance of construction firms. The relevance of the concepts outlined in the first volume have been considered here in relation to the management of large construction firms. There is however scope for a close and rigorous analysis of their relevance and applicability to *particular* firms, types of operations and functions. There is also a need to tailor the presentation of the theory to the specific characteristics of the construction industry and firms. This will not happen without a closer working relationship between academics and the industry which already exists in some of the technical, as distinct from management, areas. The solution lies in determined joint efforts by academic leaders and construction policy makers to maximise the contribution of academic research and teaching to the efficient performance of the construction industry.

NOTES AND REFERENCES

1. Hillebrandt, P.M. and Cannon, J. (eds) *The Management of Construction Firms: Aspects of Theory* (London: Macmillan, 1989 (see Appendix 1 for outline of this book).
2. Ramsay, W., 'Business Objectives and Strategy', Chapter 2 in Hillebrandt and Cannon (eds) (1989) see note 1.
3. Handy, C.B., *Understanding Organisations* (Harmondsworth: Penguin, 1988).
4. See chapters 2 and 5 of Hillebrandt and Cannon (eds) (1989) see note 1.
5. Peters, T.J. and Waterman, R.H., *In Search of Excellence* (New York: Harper & Row, 1982).
6. See note 2.
7. Cannon, J. and Hillebrandt, P.M., 'Diversification', Chapter 3 in Hillebrandt and Cannon (eds) (1989) see note 1.
8. Seymour, H., 'International Contracting', Chapter 4 in Hillebrandt and Cannon (eds) (1989) see note 1.
9. Cannon, J. and Hillebrandt, P.M., 'Financial Strategy', Chapter 5 in Hillebrandt and Cannon (eds) (1989) see note 1.
10. Male, S. and Stocks, R., 'Managers and the Organisation', Chapter 7 in Hillebrandt and Cannon (eds) (1989) see note 1.
11. Flanagan, R. and Norman, G., 'Pricing Policy', Chapter 9 in Hillebrandt and Cannon (eds) (1989) see note 1.
12. Clark, P., 'Social Technology and Structure', Chapter 6 in Hillebrandt and Cannon (eds) (1989) see note 1.
13. Buckley, P.J. and Enderwick, P., 'Manpower Management', Chapter 8 in Hillebrandt and Cannon (eds) (1989) see note 1.

Glossary

Barriers to entry   Hindrances to potential entrants to a market because of economic or non-economic advantages held by existing firms.

Contestable monopoly   Markets with only one supply but in which competitive pressures from potential entrants impose constraints on the behaviour of the supplier.

Debt/equity ratio   Debt/equity ratio, gearing and leverage all embody the same concept and all three may be used in different senses: 1. in terms of capital – the ratio of the value of debt to the value of shareholders assets; 2. the ratio of the value of debt to assets employed minus debt. Total debt may be defined to exclude short-term debt (such as to trade creditors) but to include bonds and debentures; 3. in terms of income, the ratio of the income needed to service debt to the total income of the company. The more usual interpretations are the first and second.

Firm   This term is used in economic theory to refer to any form of operating unit from a simple proprietorship to a large public company.

Gearing   See debt/equity ratio.

Internal labour market (ILM)   The situation where the allocation and pricing of labour occur primarily within the organisation.

Leverage   See debt/equity ratio.

Opportunity cost   The evaluation placed on the most highly valued of the rejected alternatives or opportunities.

Portfolio   In a financial sense, the total of the mix of different investments held. It is often also used to describe the mix of businesses in which the company operates.

Transaction costs   The costs involved in the process of buying and selling both goods and services, including manpower.

Appendix

Principal Contents of the Companion Volume, *The Management of Construction Firms: Aspects of Theory*

Subject Index

Index of Names